KU-270-069

UNCLE ARTHUR'S

BEDTIME STORIES

(SIXTH SERIES)

𝔚𝔦𝔱𝔥 𝔈𝔳𝔢𝔯𝔶 𝔊𝔬𝔬𝔡 𝔚𝔦𝔰𝔥

TO ....

FROM ....

© Autotype Fine Art Co., Ltd.

Jesus in the carpenter's shop at Nazareth.

Uncle Arthur's
BEDTIME STORIES

(Sixth Series)

By ARTHUR S. MAXWELL

"Remember now thy Creator in the
days of thy youth." Eccles. 12 : 1.

Registered at Stationers' Hall by
THE STANBOROUGH PRESS LTD.,
WATFORD, HERTS.

Contents

For the Tiny Tots

Preface

IF anyone had told us five years ago that these little books would have a sale of a million copies, be translated into many languages, and be printed in Australia, South America, Canada, Scandinavia, and the United States, we should have laughed at them. But this is what has happened and we must take this opportunity of again thanking the many friends who have sent us kind letters of appreciation from all parts of the world. We are glad to hear from all, and those who write to the address below can always be sure of a personal reply.

Some have sent us suggestions as well as thanks and we are grateful for all. This time we have tried to please those who have asked for lots of short stories. How many more could you expect than you have in this number? We have also included by request a special section for Tiny Tots.

As in others of this series, we have adhered strictly to the original plan, that of giving stories that are true to life, each one driving home some important lesson that every child needs to learn.

We want these little books to be above all else builders of character, extolling goodness and frowning upon evil, and to this end this new volume is sent out upon its mission to the children of the world.

UNCLE ARTHUR.

Copyright, 1929.
The Stanborough Press Ltd.
Watford, Herts.

© A.S.M.

Where "Bedtime Stories" come from—"Uncle Arthur" and his children.

The Twins' Desire

- - -

When I'm old as you, Daddy,
 I shall drive your car,
Down the town and back again
 Where the sweet shops are.

When I'm old as you, Daddy,
 I shall stay up late,
Never go to bed at night,
 Till it's half-past eight.

When I'm old as you, Daddy,
 I shall buy a boat,
Sail it out upon the sea,
 Get inside and float.

When I'm old as you, Daddy,
 I shall never eat
Cabbages and cauliflowers—
 Just nice things and sweet.

When I'm old as you, Daddy,
 I shall put my feet
High up on the mantelpiece
 Choose your comfy seat.

When I'm old as you, Daddy,
 Where will you be then?
Will you love me just the same?
 Come and play again?

UNCLE ARTHUR.

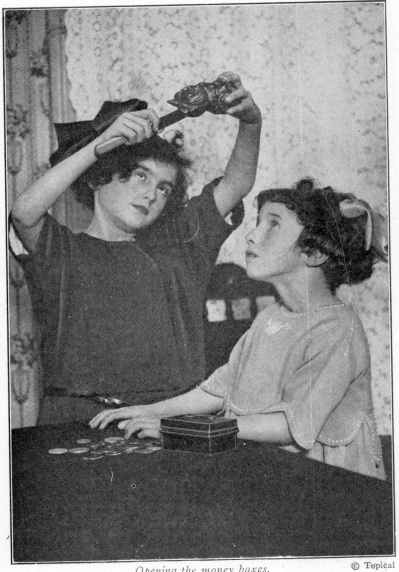

Opening the money boxes.

© Topical

How Grandma Came for Christmas

At last the day had come to open the money-boxes! How long it had taken to fill them! What hard work it had meant, what careful saving, what giving up of sweets and nice ribbons and special treats! To Hilda and Mona it had seemed as though they would never be allowed to open them and sometimes they had even said it wasn't worth while putting the money in.

But at last the day had come! It was a week before Christmas and, of course, everybody was wanting all the money they could find for presents and new dresses and things. How glad the children were that they had heeded their mother and kept the boxes unopened till now! Mother was right after all.

Click! went the key in Mona's little cash box and there inside she saw the piles of pennies, with sixpences, shillings, and one whole half-crown. What joy! She counted it all up, and Hilda counted it afterward, just to make sure it was right. Fancy! Ten shillings and threepence farthing! What a lot of money for a little girl to have!

"Now you open yours," said Mona. "I wonder who has got the most?"

Hilda's was a strange-looking money-box, but it certainly held money tightly. It was such a job to get it out. She had to use a knife, but as she poked it in, out came the pennies, threepenny bits, sixpences, shillings, and two half-crowns.

"Oh!" said Mona, "You've got much more than I have!"

"It looks like it," said Hilda. "Let's count it up. One, two, three. Why, I believe there's more than twelve shillings!"

And so there was. It came to thirteen shillings and fivepence halfpenny.

How happy they both were! Never before had they had so much money to spend all at once.

Then came the big question, What should they spend it on? Soon they realized how little they had really saved. There were so many things to buy and most of them cost more than they had both saved together.

Mona thought she would like to get a very pretty party frock, but how far would 10/3¼ go? Hilda's first thought was for a beautiful handbag, the sort with two pockets in the middle and a mirror. But again, how far would 13/5½ go? Then they talked of other things they would like, but, try as they would, they could not stretch their money nearly far enough to cover all their desires.

"I'm getting tired of trying to decide," said Hilda. "This money is a bother."

"Do you know," said Mona, "I wonder if the trouble is because we are just trying to spend it all on ourselves?"

Hilda sat very quiet and still. "Perhaps it is," she said after a while.

"Just for fun," said Mona, "let's try to think how we would spend it on some other people."

"Mamma, for instance," said Hilda.

"Yes, or even Grandma," said Mona.

"All right. You write down what you would buy for them and I'll do the same."

So they both found a pencil and paper and started to write. Hilda soon made a long list—long enough to use up her 13/5½ many times over.

"You don't seem to have put down much, Mona," she said.

"No," said Mona, "but I've got an idea. I've thought of something that would be a beautiful present both for Mamma and Grandma."

"Come on, then, let's have it," said Hilda.

"Well," said Mona, "you know how Mamma has been longing to have Grandma come down here to stay with her for a while? Well, the only reason she doesn't come is because she can't afford the fare and Mamma can't afford to send it to her. Wouldn't it be just wonderful if we were to send Grandma her fare on our own, and invite her down to surprise Mamma?"

"Mona, you are a genius!" said Hilda. "I should enjoy that much more than a new handbag. Let's do it right now."

"Isn't it just lovely!" said Mona. "I'm so glad you like the idea. I'd much rather see Mamma happy than have a new dress. Let's get a pen and some writing paper. You'll write the letter, won't you?"

"All right," said Hilda. "You tell me what to say."

So together they wrote to their grandma. The letter ran like this:

"Our dear Grandma,

"We all want you very badly to come down here

for Christmas. Mona and I have been saving up for a long time to pay your fare and you will find it in this letter. Don't lose it and be sure to come soon. We shall expect you next week.

"With lots of love from
"Hilda and Mona."

"I say, Mona," said Hilda when she had finished writing; "whatever will Mamma say when Grandma turns up?"

"Oh, that's part of the fun. She'll just be so pleased and surprised she won't know what to do with herself."

Picking up their money and putting on their hats the two wended their way down to the post office, bought a postal order for 23/-, and posted it off to Grandma. Chuckling all over, and enjoying the secret immensely, they returned home to await events.

For the next few days the girls could not settle to anything. Every footstep made them jump and every creak of the front gate gave them a start. They felt inside themselves that they had done something big and beautiful, not unmixed with mischief, and they just couldn't keep still. Every now and then they would burst out laughing, for no apparent reason whatever. Mamma wondered whatever could have gone wrong with them.

Then at last came a different knock at the door.

"Hilda, there's someone at the door," called Mamma. "Go and see who it is."

But Hilda guessed that the great moment had come and she wanted Mamma to have the surprise they had planned so long. "I really can't go," she said. "Do please go yourself, Mamma."

So Mamma hurried to the door, rather hot and

bothered, thinking it was the baker or the milkman. She opened the door sharply—and there stood Grandma, with her handbags and trunk as though she had come to stay a month.

"Good gracious!" cried Mamma. "Whoever— whatever!— Isn't this wonderful! But however did you come? Who would have dreamed you would have been here for Christmas!"

"Why, didn't you expect me?" said Grandma, equally surprised.

There was a loud chuckle in the background.

"Ah, those two young scamps," said Grandma. "I guess they are at the bottom of this."

And then came the explanations and everybody was very happy. After the excitement had died down Grandma called the children to her and opened her trunk.

"I'm not too old to use my fingers yet," she said, pulling out a couple of parcels. "Here's a little dress I've been working for Mona and I've got a wee hand-bag made all of beads for Hilda."

"Never!" cried the girls together, looking at each other in amazement.

"Why, don't you want them?" said Grandma.

"Want them! I should say we do. They are just perfect," said Hilda. "But how did you know? They are the very things we were going to buy for ourselves with the money we had saved in our boxes."

"Well, did you ever!" said Grandma. "Do you know, girls," she said, "I believe the good old Book is right when it says: 'He that hath pity upon the poor lendeth unto the Lord; and that which he hath given will He pay him again.'"

A beautiful prize pussie. © Topical

The Cat Who Paid the Bill

THIS is a true story about two boys and a cat. It happened many years ago in the city of Bath. The boys, with their mother and sister, had come over from Wales to attend some Gospel services in a big tent in the city.

The family was not well off, and money just then was very scarce. Not being able to afford many holidays they felt that this trip to Bath was something very wonderful. They enjoyed every moment.

Then one Thursday morning Mother called the boys to her and told them that she could not afford to stay any longer and that they must get ready to leave the next day.

Bertie and Willie were very disappointed and could not understand why they should have to leave while all the other people stayed. They did not think it was a bit fair and they pleaded with Mother to let them stay. But still she had to tell them that there was no money left and they would have to go.

"But can't we ask Jesus to send us the money?" said the boys. "He has plenty and surely He wants us to stay at these meetings?"

"Of course you can ask Him," said Mother; and the next morning—the very morning they were to return home—they knelt down and asked Jesus to send them £1 so that they could stay at the meetings over the week-end.

Then they left their lodgings and went to the big tent. Believing that Jesus would answer their prayer they did not tell anybody that they might have to leave that day, and they did not say good-bye to anyone.

Afternoon came. The children's meeting closed and the boys started back to their lodgings. Still no money had come. It seemed that they would have to return home after all.

Now in order to reach the house in which they were staying the boys had to cross right through the town from Beechen Cliffs to Walcot. Usually they followed the lower Walcot road, but this time departed from their custom and turned into the Paragon, a crescent of large houses.

In those days there was a cabstand on the corner of the Paragon and the children loved to play around it. As they were doing so, Bertie, who was ten years old, suddenly called to his brother.

"Willie, come and look at this!" he said, pointing to a notice stuck on the window of a doctor's house just opposite the cabstand.

Willie ran across and together they read the notice.

LOST

Valuable Persian cat. Anyone returning same to this address will receive £1 reward.

A fever of excitement seized the boys.   Fancy! £1 reward! Why, that was the very amount which they had asked Jesus to send them.   They could almost feel the money in their pockets already.   Now they could stay!   Wouldn't Mother be pleased!   The only difficulty, of course, was to find the cat.

"We must find it!" said Willie, all eagerness.

"We are going to find it!" said Bertie.

But where could it be?   It might be anywhere in Bath for ought they knew, and they had very little time to search as they were due to leave for home in an hour or two.

All along the street they talked about the possibility of finding this precious cat.   One moment it seemed impossible, the next they almost felt it purring in their arms.

They had not gone far when a sound from a dark corner brought them both to a standstill, struck dumb with excitement.

Meow!   Meow!

Willie looked at Bertie, and Bertie looked at Willie.   Could it—could it be?

They peered down into the area whence the sound had come.   To be sure, there was a cat at the bottom. They ran down the steps and found themselves face to face with a beautiful big Persian cat.   Indeed it was so big that neither of the boys could pluck up courage enough to touch it.

"It must be the doctor's cat!" they cried together. "But how shall we get it back to him?"

"You stay here and watch it," said Bertie, "while I run back to the house."

The doctor's house was only a short distance away and in a few moments Willie was back again with the doctor's servant. Yes! It was the cat that had been lost.

In great glee the boys returned to their mother to tell how Jesus had answered their prayer and that they need not go home that night.

The next day they visited the doctor, who gladly handed them the reward and thanked them for helping him to find his cat. Mother was able to cancel the arrangements to return home and they all stayed until the meetings closed.

Isn't it wonderful what Jesus will do to answer little boys' prayers?

And can you wonder that both Willie and Bertie are missionaries for Jesus in Africa to-day?

Reggie's Idea

"THESE are hard times," said Mamma, "and I'm afraid there will be no money for Christmas presents this year."

"Oh, you've said that every year," said Bessie.

"But I mean it this time," said Mamma. "We simply can't afford it. I'm very sorry, but there it is."

The children looked very despondent. Reggie and Bessie went out into the garden to talk it over.

"I don't mind so much," said Reggie, "although I was looking forward to getting some new tyres for my bicycle. What I don't like is that little May and Flo should be disappointed. They count on getting something so much. They will cry their poor little eyes out."

"Whatever happens," said Bessie, " we must see that they get something. I don't mind if I don't get those new books I wanted so long as the darlings get something to please them."

Both Reggie and Bessie loved their baby sisters very much indeed and always did everything they could to make them happy. So you can guess they could not bear the thought of the little dears waking up on Christmas morning to find their stockings empty.

"Suppose there isn't any money to spend," said Reggie bravely, "that doesn't stop us making something for them. I've got a bright idea."

"What is it? Do tell us," said Bessie.

19

"Oh!" cried little May.

© Cassell & Co.

"I'll tell you," said Reggie. "Let us two make them a fine dolls' house. They will just screech with joy at it. I can make the house and put in the doors and windows and you can make the curtains and stick the paper on the walls."

"What a splendid idea!" said Bessie. "That should not cost us a penny. Let's start right away."

"Come on, then," said Reggie, leading the way to the wood shed.

"Ah, here's a nice box," he said. "Look, the sides are all nice and smooth and it's just the right shape. All I shall have to do will be to build a roof, put a door on, and divide the inside into rooms."

"How lovely!" said Bessie. "I almost wish you were going to make it for me."

So Reggie started to work at once. He had learnt a little about using tools at school, so he knew just what to do. Very soon his wooden box was looking like a house, with a nice, pointed roof. He cut two windows in each side and made a door and four windows in the front. Of course, he made the whole front to open on hinges so that one could get at all the rooms easily. Then he painted the sides red and lined them with pencil to make them look like bricks. The top he painted grey to look like slates.

It took him a few days to finish his part of the job and then Bessie began. In the meantime she had found some rolls of wall-paper up in the loft from which she cut enough to cover the walls of the house. Then she had found some old pieces of cloth in a box upstairs that made splendid curtains and other pieces of thick material that did for rich-looking carpets on the floors. By the time her nimble fingers had finished, the inside of the house looked really pretty. But it was bare of furniture.

So Reggie got busy again. Out of some empty match-boxes he made a splendid chest of drawers, with drawers that really opened and closed. A piece of polished tin, cut into an oval shape with Mamma's old scissors, did for a mirror. A square piece of wood and four legs soon made a table and it did not take a great while to make some chairs to match it. Before long, indeed, Reggie had the house furnished from top to bottom and it really did look nice. When it was all done they shut the big shed door and waited for Christmas morning.

It came at last. Very early, while the two little girls were still sleeping, Reggie and Bessie brought in the beautiful dolls' house and placed it on the bottom of their bed. As they were doing so one of them accidentally kicked the iron bedpost and—up jumped little May.

She rubbed her eyes in astonishment and shouted "Oh!" That woke little Flo, who promptly sat up in bed and yelled with delight.

"What a beautiful house!" they cried. "Is it Bessie's?"

"No, it's for you—both of you," said Bessie. "Reggie and I have made it for you. Why, don't you know, this is Christmas day and this is the beautiful surprise we have been saving for you!"

"Oh, how lovely!" cried the little girls together as they jumped out of bed and threw their arms first round Bessie's and then round Reggie's neck.

As for Reggie and Bessie the joy of that moment more than made up for all the trouble they had taken over making the house and in their happiness they quite forgot that Father Christmas had passed them by this year.

They had discovered the truth of that saying of Jesus: "It is more blessed to give than to receive."

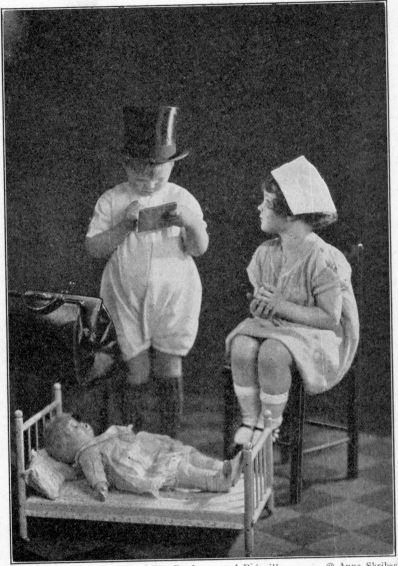

Dr. Pills, Barbara, and Priscilla.　　© Anne Shriber

Poor Priscilla

"OH dear!" cried Barbara, wringing her hands, "What can be the matter with Priscilla? I must fetch the doctor at once."

So, laying poor Priscilla down on her pretty white bedstead, Barbara went over to the electric light switch and pretended that it was the telephone.

"Hallo! Is that you, Dr. Pills?"

"Yes, madam," came a voice from the other side of the door. "This is Dr. Pills. What can I do for you?"

"Oh doctor, my poor Priscilla has been taken so ill. Please do come at once."

"I will come at once," said the voice in the corridor. "My car is waiting at the gate so I shall only be a few moments."

Barbara returned to Priscilla's bedside and tried hard to weep some tears over her. There was a knock at the door.

"Ah, so here you are, Dr. Pills. I'm so glad you've come."

Dr. Pills, wearing Father's top-hat and carrying his handbag, walked over to the bed. He tried to look very serious.

"Let me feel her pulse," he said, taking Priscilla's hand. "Ah, very fast, very fast," he murmured.

"Poor Priscilla!" said Barbara.

"Now let me look at her tongue," said Dr. Pills.

"I'm afraid she's too ill to open her mouth," said Barbara. "Do tell me what you think is the matter."

"A very serious case," said Dr. Pills. "Very serious."

"Oh, what shall I do, what shall I do?" cried Barbara.

"Do?" said Dr. Pills. "There is only one thing to do. You must treat the child better. You have been feeding her wrongly. She has acute indigestion and will probably die."

"Die, oh dear! How terrible!" exclaimed Barbara. "What should I feed her on to make her well and strong again?"

"Ahem!" said Dr. Pills. "Let me see. This child has been eating too many sweets. She has been eating them all day long and has ruined her stomach. You must stop giving her sweets, except at meals."

"But she will cry so!" said Barbara.

"Never mind," said Dr. Pills. "Better cry than die. Children must not eat between meals. It is very bad for them. And, let me see, does she eat plenty of greens?"

"Oh no, doctor. She hates greens. Whenever I bring them on the table she grumbles terribly."

"Never mind," said Dr. Pills sternly. "Better grumble than be ill. She must eat some greens every day. Lettuces, cabbages, sprouts, cauliflowers, and things like that, you know."

"Not all of them every day!"

"Oh dear, no!" said Dr. Pills. "But one of them at least every day. And let me see, does the child get enough fruit?"

"She likes bananas and pears, but, you know, they are so expensive I can't afford to give her very many."

"She must have plenty of fruit. Stop giving her

sugary cakes and pastries and give her apples and oranges instead."

"I once heard," said Barbara, "that an apple a day keeps the doctor away. Is there any truth in it?"

"Certainly," said Dr. Pills. "I shall never have to come back again if you do that—unless, of course, she catches measles or scarlet fever."

"Oh, thank you so much, Dr. Pills," said Barbara. "How much is your fee?"

"My fee?" said Dr. Pills. "My fee is ten shillings and sixpence."

"Rather high, isn't it?" said Barbara, taking ten big buttons and six little buttons out of her purse.

"My usual charge, thank you," said Dr. Pills. "Thank you. I trust your daughter will soon be better. And mind you follow my instructions."

"I will," said Barbara, as she closed the door. "But, I say," she called. "Peter, you won't forget to put Father's hat back in the proper place, will you?"

"What's behind those big brown eyes?" © Anne Shriber

Gladys Greatheart

"WHAT'S behind those big brown eyes, Gladys dear?" asked Mamma, as she crept quietly up beside her little daughter.

"I'm thinking," said Gladys.

"You're always thinking," said Mamma.

"Am I?" she said, going off into dreamland again.

Gladys loved to go down the garden all by herself and sit on a log or a pile of grass and plan beautiful things, or count the ants at her feet, or lie on her back and watch the clouds go by. Then she would come indoors again, bringing sunshine and happiness everywhere she went. Nothing pleased her more than to gather flowers for the table, or run messages for Mamma, or have Daddy's slippers ready for him just in the right place when he came home. That's why they called her Gladys Greatheart.

"What's behind the clouds, Mamma?" she asked, after a little while.

"The big blue sky," said Mamma.

"And what's behind the big blue sky?"

"The stars."

"And what's behind the stars, Mamma?"

"More stars," said Mamma.

"And what's behind the more stars?"

"Ah, that's where God lives."

"How far away He must be!"

"It seems a long way to us, but it's not far to Him," said Mamma. "He can travel so swiftly, you

29

see. He could come all the way from His home to ours in less than a second."

"What about the stars in the way?"

"Oh, He knows the way here."

"Do you think He has time to think about us?"

"I'm sure He does. And He loves us very much and wants us to be good and kind as He is."

"And does He love all the little children in the world?"

"All of them, just the same. You see, they all belong to Him, so they are all just one big family in His sight."

"What a lot of brothers and sisters I must have!"

"Yes," said Mamma, "hundreds and thousands of them. And God wants us to love them all as He does, and to be kind to them, especially to the poor and sick and those who cannot care for themselves."

Gladys thought for quite a long time.

"Peggy is sick," she said, breaking the silence. "May I take her my painting book this afternoon? And the brush, of course."

"If you wish," said Mamma. "I am sure Jesus would be pleased."

"Do you think He will know about it?"

"Oh yes. The angels will tell Him at once, and all heaven will be happier."

"Do you really think so?"

"Oh yes," said Mamma. "It's just as though you gave it right into His own hand, for He said one time, long ago, 'Inasmuch as ye have done it unto one of the least of these, My children, ye have done it unto Me.' "

"I think I will take that nice pincushion you made

me as well, Mamma. I think Peggy would like to play with that too."

So they planned to visit Peggy; and from Peggy they went to others who were sick and poor, scattering joy and gladness along their pathway and making friends with the children of the God Who made the skies.

And when Jesus comes back through the stars to take His people to their heavenly home, I think He will want to take Gladys Greatheart with Him too, don't you?

Playing shops.   © P. Phillips, Ipswich

Muriel's Customer

LITTLE Muriel was a very lonely little girl. Her mother had been taken very ill and sent to a hospital and she had come to stay with her auntie.

She liked being with her auntie all right, but there was no one to play with. Auntie was getting old and seemed to have forgotten that she had ever been a child herself. Muriel was sure she didn't understand little girls. She was always saying, "Please do be quiet, Muriel," and, "Don't get up to mischief, Muriel," until poor Muriel didn't know just what to do to be good.

One day Auntie got an idea. "When I was a little girl," she said, "we used to play shops."

"I'd like to play shops," said Muriel, glad to find something at last that Auntie thought was "being good."

So Auntie allowed Muriel to take some wooden boxes out into the garden and some old tins that had once contained such goodies as toffee and butterscotch.

For a little while Muriel was very happy arranging the counter, but when that was done she began to get lonesome again, for what is the good of a shop if there is no one to buy your goods?

So she got one of her old dolls and stuck it up in front of the counter and pretended that the doll was a customer. But a doll is a very unsatisfactory sort of customer. For one thing she will not take the things away and for another she will not pay for them.

So poor Muriel soon got tired of that and dismissed the doll from the shop.

"Oh dear!" she sighed.   "I do wish someone would come to play with me!"

Hardly had she spoken than a nice tabby cat walked slowly round the corner of the shop and jumped up on a box in front of the counter.

"Well, you are a nice customer!" said Muriel, smiling for the first time that afternoon.   "And what would you like to buy to-day, Mr. Pusscat?"

"A pennyworth of sugar," said Mr. Pusscat as well as he could, opening his mouth wide and getting rather too near the sugar bag for safety.

Muriel guessed what he meant, and held up a piece of sugar to see if she had guessed rightly.

Mr. Pusscat opened his mouth wider still and swallowed the lump of sugar with relish.   Evidently Muriel had not been mistaken.

"But now, Mr. Pusscat, how about paying for it?" said Muriel sternly.   "Nobody is allowed to take things from this shop without paying for them, you know."

Mr. Pusscat raised his right foot as though about to pass over the necessary money, and Muriel took the will for the deed.

Well, they had great times together.   So long as the supply of sugar lasted, Mr. Pusscat was a regular customer and Muriel succeeded in selling him quite a number of other things as well.   He came back the next day and they started all over again.   Muriel got a bright idea and decided to enlarge her shop and add a dairy.   Mr. Pusscat strongly approved and came back frequently to purchase saucerfuls of milk.   The only trouble was to get Auntie to understand why **so** much milk was needed in the shop.

So in a very little while Muriel and Mr. Pusscat became great friends. He would follow her about everywhere she went, and even when Auntie took her shopping Mr. Pusscat would follow behind like a little dog. They played together all day long and in her love for pussy Muriel forgot her loneliness.

Then one day a letter came to say that Mother was better and **Muriel** could go home again. She didn't know whether to laugh for joy at the thought of going home or cry for sadness at parting from her new-found friend.

© P. Phillips, Ipswich

"A pennyworth of sugar," said Mr. Pusscat.

So she played one last game of shops and sold Mr. Pusscat all the milk he could drink and all the sugar he could eat, and didn't charge him anything for it either. Then she said good-bye with tears running down her cheeks.

Auntie said it was very foolish for a little girl to cry over a cat, especially when she ought to be so thankful that her mother was better, but Muriel just couldn't help it.

Soon she was home again and so glad to see her Mamma well and strong once more. But somehow she couldn't forget her friend, and longed to have him with her.

Then one morning, what do you suppose happened?

Well, it was her birthday, and when she got downstairs she saw a strange-looking parcel beside her plate on the breakfast table. Quickly she removed the paper. Underneath was a basket, and in the basket was—

Mr. Pusscat.

So Auntie had understood after all!

Daddy's Discovery

Ronald returned from school one day looking very sick. As he came indoors he walked across the dining-room and flopped into an arm-chair.

"Whatever's the matter, Ronny?" asked Mother. "You don't look very well."

"Don't feel well," said Ronald.

"What have you been eating at school?" asked Mother.

"Haven't eaten anything since dinner," said Ronny. "I just feel sick. Don't worry. I'll be better to-morrow."

"Well, tea is nearly ready."

"Don't want any tea."

"What do you want?"

"Oh, nothing. I think I'll go to bed early."

"Daddy will be back at seven; better wait till then; he likes to find you here."

"No," said Ronald, "I shall go before that to-night." And so saying he went upstairs, and from the noises overhead Mother guessed that he was getting undressed right away.

At seven Daddy came in. "Where's Ronald?" he asked.

"In bed," said Mother.

"In bed!" repeated Daddy with surprise. "Whatever for? I'll go up and see him."

Daddy bounded upstairs and into Ronald's room.

"What's the matter, Son?" he asked.

Ronald pretended to be asleep, but Daddy knew a

thing or two about that, having tried the same trick himself sometimes when he was a little boy.

"Come on now, Ronny. You're not asleep. What's the matter?"

"Feeling sick," murmured Ronny.

"Let me feel your pulse."

Ronny held out his hand. Daddy felt his pulse and noticed something.

"What's this on your fingers, Son?"

Ronny pulled his hand into bed. "Nothing Dad, paint, I think."

"Let me see your tongue."

Ronald opened his mouth. Daddy bent down very close, much closer than he really needed just to look in. Then he got up from the bed, and walked over to the chair where Ronald's clothes were lying. He picked them up one by one and felt carefully in the pockets. It was rather a messy job, for some of the pockets had all sorts of treasures in them, such as bits of string, nails, conkers, dirty handkerchiefs, a half-melted toffee, an apple core, and biscuit crumbs. But from the bottom of the right-hand trouser pocket Daddy hauled out a small yellow box.

He came back to Ronny, who had been lying very quiet and still during the search.

"Ronny, why have you these matches in your pocket?"

"To light fireworks," said Ronny quietly.

"Are you sure, Ronny?" said Daddy very solemnly. "Are you really telling me the truth?"

There was a long silence.

"Tell me," said Daddy, "was that the truth?"

"No," said Ronald, very, very quietly.

"I knew it wasn't," said Daddy. "Directly I saw

your hand and smelt your breath I knew you had been playing with tobacco. Am I right?"

"Yes, a boy at school dared me to try it," said Ronald, tears streaming down his cheeks.

"Oh Ronny! I am so sorry," said Daddy. "I had hoped you would never learn that horrid, dirty, wasteful habit. I have never smoked tobacco in my life, and

© Anne Shriber

Boys who want to be strong and well should never smoke.

I wanted my son never, never to have anything to do with it."

"I knew you didn't, Daddy, and I really didn't want to," said Ronny amid his tears.

"I'm sure you didn't," said Daddy. "But you must be strong next time to say No! Smoking never did anybody any good. It spoils your health, weakens your heart, stains your hands, makes your breath smell, and burns up your money."

Daddy paused, and there was a deep silence, broken only by Ronny's deep breathing and an occasional sob.

"Ronny!" said Daddy.

"Yes, Daddy."

"I want you to promise me one thing."

"Yes, Daddy."

"Give me your hand."

Ronny put it out.

"Promise me," said Daddy, taking the little hand in his, "promise me that you will never put tobacco of any kind near your mouth again."

"I promise," said Ronny.

They squeezed hands in the darkness and the promise was sealed.

Starving Mothers

I READ a most remarkable story the other day about a poor mother who nearly died of starvation.

Was she living on a desert island? Oh no.

Did she belong to a home where the father was out of work and no money was coming in? No.

This mother lived in a good house in a nice suburb of London. The father earned good money and there was a family of strong, healthy children.

Then, you say, how could the mother have nearly starved to death?

But it's true she nearly did.

Noticing that Mother was not looking well, the eldest daughter took her to see the doctor. And what do you think the doctor said?

He said, "My girl, your mother is being starved. You go home and watch."

Starved! The girl could not believe it. Starved in the midst of plenty! It seemed impossible.

But the girl did watch. And what do you think she noticed?

Well, she just listened and looked on at dinner-time.

Mother brought in the dinner. At once voices began to cry out.

"I don't like this," said one. "I don't want that," said another. "I'm going to have that nice piece over there," said a third. "You've got a bigger bit than I have," said a fourth.

The hubbub was terrible, and poor Mother, weary

with everybody's grumbling, gave away the best of everything she had prepared. She was left with what everybody else didn't want. The last remnants of the dishes were hers. She was literally starving herself that the others might be happy.

Well, the eldest daughter watched this go on for a while and then she began to speak; and she told the rest of the family just what she thought of them. And, do you know, they all said they had never noticed it before! They were all so anxious to get just what they wanted for themselves they had never had a thought about Mother.

But once they realized what was happening, all was changed. All of them said at once, "Why, of course, Mother must have the best of everything. Mother works the hardest, so Mother should be fed the best."

And so that poor, starved mother at last began to get what she deserved. She was served first instead of last. The children waited on her instead of her waiting on them. She was given the softest chair instead of being allowed to sit on the hardest. She was made to eat the choicest portions of every dish instead of the last remnants after the others had been satisfied.

And so she began to get better; and I am sure everybody in that family was happier for being less selfish.

But I wonder how many other mothers are being starved in the midst of plenty. Why not have a look and see how your mother is getting along?

Those Gooseberries

GERALD was very fond of gooseberries. In fact, he was so fond of them when they were nearly ripe that it was difficult for him to walk down the garden without picking one. Did I say one? I should have said several; for unless someone were looking, Gerald, I am sorry to say, would pick as many as his little hands and pockets could carry.

Now it so happened that Mother also was fond of gooseberries, to say nothing of Father, who liked to walk up and down amongst the bushes now and then, trying the flavour of one or two off each bush.

One day Daddy went down the garden for a stroll, hoping to have a fat, juicy gooseberry or two when he got down to the bushes.

But when he got there, the bushes were bare. There was not a gooseberry to be seen. Even the very big one that had been growing all by itself and which Daddy had been watching with such pride and anticipation, had disappeared. The trees had been stripped as completely as if a great wind had blown over them and swept all the gooseberries away.

"I wonder who could have taken all the gooseberries?" said Daddy to himself. "It surely could not have been Gerald, for I've spoken to him so many times about picking them. Perhaps the birds have been at them again, or maybe Mamma has picked them for jam."

Just then a cheery voice called from the other end of the garden.

"Hallo, Daddy! Come and look at my garden."
It was Gerald.

Daddy walked over to the little patch which had been given over to the boy to cultivate.

"Look, Dad, see these lovely flowers. Aren't they fine?"

"I should think so," said Dad. "Nice apples you've got, too."

"Rather," said Gerald. "And I hope nobody picks them but me."

"Particular about it, aren't you?" said Daddy.

"I should say I am," said Gerald. "Here I've waited all the year for them, manured the tree and watered it and kept the weeds from it—I should think I **am** particular about who picks the apples. If Baby touches them I'll give him a good hiding."

"I see," said Daddy, his eyes wandering over the rest of Gerald's garden and lighting on a pile of strange green objects lying partly concealed by a cabbage leaf.

Gerald, noticing the direction of Daddy's gaze, promptly put his foot on the cabbage leaf and began to talk about his sunflowers.

"Big sunflower that, isn't it?" he said, blushing a little.

But Daddy was not interested in sunflowers. He had become exceedingly interested in cabbages.

"Nice cabbages these," he said. "You have done well, Gerald. Do let me feel the heart of this one. You shouldn't tread on the leaves of such fine plants."

Gerald blushed more deeply as Daddy bent down to "feel" the plant.

"I didn't know that you had any gooseberry

bushes in your garden," said Daddy rather sternly as he stood up again.

"I haven't," said Gerald very faintly and blushing more deeply.

"Then where did these skins come from?" asked Daddy.

"Down the garden," said Gerald.

"I'm sorry," said Daddy. "I thought I could trust my boy. Don't you think it was very mean of you to take all those gooseberries when you knew how we have been waiting all the year for them? Haven't you seen me down there by the hour weeding them and pruning them and manuring them?"

Gerald seemed to recognize his own argument and looked very sorry for himself.

"It's too bad," said Daddy. "And somehow you must learn not to do it again. Seeing you have helped yourself to my gooseberries I think I will try a few of your apples."

So Daddy began to pick the ripest of them.

"No, no, no!" cried Gerald, bursting into tears. "You mustn't pick my apples! They're mine! I've grown them all myself!"

"But what about my gooseberries?" said Daddy, proceeding to eat the fattest and rosiest apple. If we say six gooseberries equal one apple I should think I am entitled to all the apples on this tree."

"But you mustn't pick them all!" cried Gerald frantically.

"I won't, on one condition."

"What's that?" asked Gerald.

"That you promise never again to take things that do not belong to you."

"All right. I'll promise it," said Gerald.

"Yes," said Daddy, "and remember what the Golden Rule says about doing unto others as you would like them to do unto you."

Gerald tried hard to remember and next year he picked his own apples, while Daddy had all the gooseberries he desired.

Robert's Mistake

"Do let me go down to the creek, Mother," said Robert. "All the boys are going to-day."

"Not to-day, dearie. I'm sorry," said Mother. "You know how ill you have been."

"Yes, I know, but I'm quite better now."

"Not quite; but if you are very careful you will be all right next week."

"Oh, do let me go!" coaxed Robert.

"I wouldn't mind your just walking down there if I were sure you wouldn't bathe," said Mother, anxious to please the boy as far as possible.

"Oh, that's all right," said Robert. "You needn't worry about that. I won't bathe till next week."

"Then on that condition you can go."

"Oh, thank you!" shouted Robert, as he bounded out of the house and ran down the lane towards the creek.

The tide was up and the creek was full. Bright sunshine beat down on the calm waters. An old sailing boat tugged gently at its moorings as the tide moved lazily by. It was a scene to stir any boy's heart.

"Hurrah! Here's old Robert again!" cried a group of boys who were bathing in the creek and obviously enjoying themselves to the full. "Come on, Robert! It's just grand. Get your things off!"

"Sorry, chaps, but I can't bathe to-day. I haven't brought my bathing suit."

"I'll lend you mine," cried the cheery little voice

Bathing in the creek.

© Topical

of Teddy Brown. "I'm just going in anyway. I've been soaking in this pool all day."

"Afraid I can't," said Robert. "Mother said I mustn't."

"Oh, Mummie's, Mummie's darling!" sang a voice from the creek and all the other boys took it up.

Poor Robert blushed and began to feel more and more uncomfortable.

"I'll come in next week," he said, "but not now."

"You're afraid!" said someone.

"He can't swim!" said another.

"He thinks we'll duck him!" said a third.

Robert's determination began to waver. After all, he felt quite well. Why shouldn't he just have a little dip? The water was warm. He could just go in for a few minutes and come out again. That would at least show the boys that he was not a coward. And how would Mother know anything about it anyway?

He began to take off his coat.

"Hip-hip-hooray!" shouted the boys. "Good old Robert! Let's give him a splash!"

It did not take Robert more than a minute to get out of his clothes and into Teddy Brown's bathing suit, wet and clammy as it was.

But once in the water he did not feel quite so happy as he had expected to be. Neither did he feel so well. And when the boys had finished splashing him he was not a little tired. He thought he would have a little swim out into the creek before going in. But he had not gone far before he felt sharp pains in his legs. It was the dreaded cramp.

"Help!" he cried. In a moment half a dozen boys were swimming towards him. They soon dragged him back to the landing place and rubbed his legs

VI B.S. 4

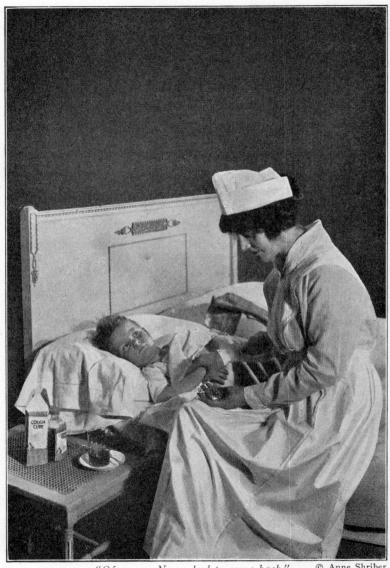

"Of course Nurse had to come back."   © Anne Shriber

until he was able to stand up again. Then they all helped him on with his clothes.

"I shouldn't have gone in," he said. "I've been ill and am only just better."

"Why didn't you say so?" said Teddy. "We wouldn't have teased you if we'd known. Now we'd better see you home."

"No, don't," said Robert, a new fear entering his heart. "I'll go by myself."

Mother was out when he reached home, so he slunk in at the back door and up to bed. He was feeling distinctly unwell. All the strength he had thought he had in the morning seemed to have gone. He felt as bad as he had done a week before.

"Hallo!" said Mother in surprise as she came into his room on her return. "In bed again! I thought you were having a nice stroll down by the creek."

"I was," said Robert, "but—er—I came over sick and thought I had better come home. And as you were out I thought bed was the best place."

"That's too bad," said Mother. "I thought we had got you almost well again."

"Let me feel your head," she said. "You look feverish again."

Mother placed her hand on Robert's forehead— and the secret was out.

"Robert!"

Robert understood.

"Robert, your hair is wet."

"I'm sorry, Mother."

"Why did you do it?"

"The boys said I was a coward not to go in."

"A coward! Don't you think you were a bigger coward for giving way to them?"

"I know; but I thought you wouldn't hear about it."

"But, Robert, don't you remember the Bible says, 'Be sure your sin will find you out'?"

"Yes," said Robert, "and it has found me out this time again."

"And it always will," said Mother.

Of course the nurse had to come back, and she said that poor Robert must stay in bed another fortnight. He was dreadfully disappointed, but at least it gave him time to think over what had happened and to resolve never to disobey Mother again.

The Angel of the Books

"WHAT dreadful language you are bringing into this house, Tom," said Mother one day. "Why, even Joan and Jess are calling each other 'little beasts' and things like that. It's got to stop."

"Can't help it," said Tom, who had just started going to school. "All the boys call each other names."

"But you mustn't do it, Tom. You must be different and set the other boys a good example."

"Can't," said Tom. "They're all bigger than I am and they won't listen to me."

"That may be," said Mamma, "but you don't need to use the same language as the other boys. Anyhow, you mustn't use it in this house, that's all."

"Oh blow!" said Tom.

"Tom!" exclaimed Mother. "That's the last time you have said that here."

"Oh blow!" came an echo from the dining-room.

"There!" said Mother. "There's little Joan learning that from you now. I won't have it. The next time you use any of those idle words you shall go straight to bed without any tea."

"Beastly mean!" muttered Tom under his breath.

"That's enough," said Mother. "Up you go."

"But I was just going out to play football."

"Doesn't matter. It is much more important that you learn that you must not use bad language."

Tom sauntered slowly upstairs and into his bedroom. More slowly still he undressed and got into bed. He didn't mind going to bed so much, but the fact that there was to be no tea was too much for him. Tears began to trickle down his cheeks. He tossed and turned, wiped his eyes, put the handkerchief under his pillow, and pulled it out again. Gradually he dozed off.

Hallo! Who was this in his bedroom? He rubbed his eyes and sat up, very frightened.

"Who are you?" he asked.

"I am the Angel of the Books," said the visitor.

"Books!" gasped Tom. "What books?"

"The books of heaven," said the angel. "I record every idle word that men speak."

"Good Lor'," said Tom.

"That also will be written down."

"Mustn't I say that?"

"It is very wrong. Have you not read, 'Thou shalt not take the name of the Lord thy God in vain'?"

"I'm sorry," said Tom. "I won't say it any more."

"You will not be able to," said the angel. "You have said so many bad words of late that you must be silent for a long time. Good-bye."

The angel disappeared. Tom, very frightened, tried to call Mother and tell her all about what he had seen. But he could not speak. It was terrible. He wanted to tell Mother how sorry he was for being rude to her, but he couldn't say a word. He remembered how mean he had been to his Auntie and wanted to go and ask her pardon, but not a word could he utter. Then he thought of dear little Jess and Joan. How he wanted to go and tell them a story and be nice to them to make up for teasing them so much. But he could not. Not a word would come from his lips.

"Oh dear!" he thought. "Shall I never be able to speak again?"

He saw Mother lying in bed very ill and heard the doctor come and say how sick she was. He heard people come upstairs bringing fruit and flowers to cheer her up. He heard all the kind things they said to her. How he longed to go to her bedside and tell her he would try to be a good boy and how he, too, wanted her to be well again. But his tongue would not move.

Ah! Here was the angel back again.

"I believe you have learned your lesson," said the Angel of the Books.

Tom nodded his head, while tears ran down his face.

"If you promise to try hard never to use a bad word again," said the angel, "you may speak."

Tom nodded his head, the gift of speech returned, and the angel disappeared once more.

* * * * * * *

"Whatever's the matter, dearie?" said Mother, bending over him.

"Oh, Mother dear!" cried Tom. "I've had such a wonderful and terrible dream. And I do love you so much and I'll never, never use bad words again."

The lighthouse on the shore.

© Topical

The Lighthouse Children

FAR away on a rocky shore stood a lighthouse. Night after night its brilliant beam shone out across the dark and treacherous waters.

Slowly the light turned, growing brighter, then fainter, then brighter again, never failing, ever warning of the rocks that lay beneath. Ships that passed in the night understood, and sailed in safety into the harbour.

Winter and summer the light blazed on. Through long, calm, starlit nights, through storm and tempest, it never went out. The deeper the darkness the more brilliantly it shone; the more terrible the tempest the more welcome were its warning beams.

In that far-off, lonely lighthouse lived a man, his wife, and two children, Paul and Rene. It was a quiet and strange life for them. Their home was the tall, narrow lighthouse. Their life centred in the light above them. They were there for the one purpose of keeping the light burning.

One evening, as dusk was falling, Father climbed up the steep, narrow staircase, as he had done so many times before, to kindle the light. In a few moments he returned, looking pale and sick.

"I am ill," he said, and collapsed in a chair.

Mother ran to him in deep distress for it was clear he was dying. For a moment all was confusion and the children stood by anxious and worried.

57

After a little while, when Father had been put to bed, Paul spoke.

"Mother," he said. "What about the light?"

"Go and see," she said, "I cannot go now."

So Paul and Rene crept softly out of the little room and climbed up the cold, dark staircase.

Night had fallen. A storm was blowing up, dark clouds scudded across the pale moon. Below, great waves boomed on the rocks, the spray hissing uncannily as it fell back into the wild sea.

The light was burning, but there was something wrong. Over the sea all was darkness, and the great beam from the lighthouse shone only towards the land.

"Rene!" cried Paul, "The shade is not turning. The ships will never see the light."

"Can you start the machinery?" asked Rene.

"I'll try," said Paul.

Paul had seen his father do it many times and thought he could do it now. But he soon found that something was the matter; something had gone wrong. A piece of the machinery was broken and he could not mend it.

"What shall we do?" cried Rene.

"There is the hand wheel left," said Paul.

"But you could not turn that alone."

"No, but we could turn it together," said Paul. "Remember, Rene, we are the children of the light."

"I'll help you," cried Rene.

Seizing the great hand wheel they began to turn. The shade of the light moved, and they were glad. The ships would see the light after all.

Hour after hour they toiled on. No night had ever seemed so long. Their little hands became sore and blistered. Their little arms grew tired. Minutes seemed like hours and hours like years. They grew so weary that they wept as they turned. Outside the storm broke and raged in fury around them. Below, Father was dying and Mother was weeping in sorrow over him. But still these children of the light kept turning, turning, turning. In utter weariness and sorrow they carried on until a faint grey light in the east told them that their task was done.

Captains saw the light that night and thanked God for it. Yet they never knew what was happening in the lighthouse, nor of the heroism of those two little children who were faithful to their trust.

And just as Paul and Rene kept the light burning through the long, stormy night, so God wants every child of His to keep the light of His love shining out into the cold, dark world. The darker our surroundings, the more brightly our light should shine. The worse the storm, the more constant it should be. Neither sorrow nor weariness should be allowed to put it out. There are many ships passing, looking to us for comfort and guidance and friendliness. So we who are children of the light must keep it burning through the night.

Litter left in a London park one Sunday afternoon! © Topical

Tom's Thoughtlessness

IT was a half-holiday and Tom was spending it with some of his school friends in the park.

They had all brought their lunch and after playing touch and many other games they sat down under a fine old oak tree to enjoy the good things their mothers had packed up for them.

Soon they had finished and for want of something better to do they began throwing the banana skins and orange peel at each other and scattering their lunch papers all over the place.

All of a sudden from behind the oak tree came an elderly gentleman. He made as if to go past the boys, but, stepping on one of the banana skins, he fell heavily to the ground.

Tom sprang to his side in a moment and did his best to help him to his feet again.

"I hope you're not hurt, sir," he said.

"I think not," said the gentleman. "Just a little shaken. I think I will sit on your seat for a little while if I may."

Tom helped him across to the seat and the boys stood around to see if the gentleman had hurt himself or not.

"I think I'm all right," he said, "but I'm getting on now and a fall like that is dangerous for one of my age. It's too bad that people are so careless with their banana skins, isn't it?"

"Yes," said Tom, but with rather a guilty look at the other boys.

"I hope you boys never throw banana skins about."

"Um," said Tom, blushing a little.

"So selfish, isn't it?" went on the elderly gentleman.

"I suppose it is," said Tom.

"If people only thought of the pain they might cause others I'm sure they would never do it."

"No," said Tom.

"And look at all that paper lying about," said the elderly gentleman. "Some lazy, thoughtless people must have been about here."

"Yes," said Tom, for there was nothing else he could say.

"If only," went on the gentleman, "if only people would stop to think about others they would never leave a mess like this behind them, would they?"

"No," said Tom, getting more uncomfortable.

"You know," said the gentleman, "this is a beautiful park, but if everyone left a mess like this it wouldn't be worth coming to. If it were all covered with dirty paper and orange peel and banana skins, why, you boys wouldn't want to play here, would you?"

"No fear," said Tom and the rest together.

"Well, boys, I'm feeling better now. Thank you for helping me up. I'll be off again, I think. Here's something for you, Sonnie, to get some sweets."

And so saying, to Tom's amazement, he handed him sixpence and walked away.

The boys looked at each other.

"I thought we should have got into a row," said one.

"He didn't see us," said another.

"Don't you believe it,"said Tom, "I believe he saw everything we did."

"Anyhow, he was a jolly good sport," said a third.

"And I liked what he said," said Tom. "He was so awfully decent about it."

"You're right," said another. "And that's the last time I'm going to throw stuff about here."

"I feel the same way," said Tom, and so saying he began to pick up some of the litter he had so carelessly scattered about a little while before. Strangely enough, the other boys got the same idea. They didn't say much to each other while they were doing it, but within a few minutes all the banana skins, orange peel and lunch paper had been picked up and dropped into one of the park waste-paper baskets.

"Well," said Tom, as he led the others off to the sweet shop to spend his sixpence, "I don't think we'll litter this place up again."

"Rather not!" chorused the others.

And they didn't.

"She got on board and the boat sailed off."

© Topical

How Cross Katie Became Katie the Kindhearted

You have already guessed that Katie had a very bad temper. She was always being cross. Really, you never saw anything like it. If she were asked to lay the breakfast table she grumbled; if she were given porridge instead of Granose she pouted; if Baby Brother were given a little more milk than she had, she said it wasn't fair. And so on all through the day.

The only time Katie seemed to be happy was when she was having her own way and doing just what she liked. If anybody interrupted her play—well, you should just have heard what she said.

Katie was playing with her dolls' pram, and she liked to do that very much, of course.

Along came Baby Brother.

"Do up my shoes, please, Katie," he said.

"Can't," said Katie. "I'm busy. You'll have to wait. You're always wanting someone to tie up your shoes."

"Boo-hoo-hoo!" wailed Baby Brother, and ran off to tell Mamma.

A few minutes later the kitchen window opened and out popped Mamma's head.

"Katie, I want you to run down to the corner shop for me."

"Oh dear!" exclaimed Katie. "I'm always having to go down to that shop. I never get any time to myself."

But Katie went, muttering to herself all the way down to the front gate. She seemed to forget that Mamma was "always" doing things for her, from early morning till late at night.

When Daddy came home in the evening Katie was painting pictures in a book.

"Hallo, Katie," cried Daddy. "Fetch my slippers, there's a dear."

"Oh dear!" cried Katie again. "I'm always having to fetch things. I have been fetching things all day. I never can get time to paint these pictures."

"Oh, that's it, is it?" said Daddy, who knew Katie's weakness only too well. "It's all right; I'll fetch them myself."

So Daddy fetched his slippers and then brought one of them rather closer to a certain part of Katie than she liked. Just so that Katie wouldn't forget he did it two or three times and then sent her up to bed.

Well, Katie went upstairs, weeping copiously, and feeling crosser than ever. She planned how she would run away from home and go to some place where she wouldn't always have to be doing things for other people. The idea seemed very pleasant, and while she was thinking about it she dropped off to sleep.

While asleep she went on with her plans for running away. She got her money box, slipped downstairs, and took a bus to the station. There she got a ticket and went to a place where there was a big boat. She got on board and the boat sailed off. She travelled for a long, long time and finally reached a beautiful country where everybody could do as they liked. She got off, and the boat sailed away. For a time she was very happy. But the people were strange. She didn't know any of them and after a while she began to feel lonely. They were all doing things just for themselves and Katie found that none of them wanted to do anything for her. She thought she would like to see Mamma again. But the people told her that she couldn't go away for a long, long time as the boat wouldn't come back.

Days and weeks and months and years passed by, and then at last the boat came back and Katie jumped on board. She had been so lonely, and she was longing to go back home and see Mamma and Daddy and Baby Brother again.

Well, she got back home and walked up to the front door. She thought she would like to give Mamma a surprise. But a strange lady came to the door. An awful fear gripped Katie's heart.

"Is Mamma in?" she asked.

"Mamma? Whose mamma?" said the lady.

"My mamma!" cried Katie frantically, trying to push past the lady.

"She doesn't live here," said the lady. "The lady who used to live here died a long time ago. She was so sorry she lost her little girl."

"Mamma dead!" cried Katie. "And where's Daddy?"

"Gone away; I don't know where he is now," said the lady.

"And Baby Brother? Where is he?"

"Baby Brother? You mean your big brother. He's grown up now and gone away, too."

"Oh dear! Oh dear!" cried poor little Katie. "They've all gone! Oh, why did I run away! If only they would come back again, how I would love them! I'm sure I'd never be cross with them any more. Oh Mamma, Mamma, do come back again!"

"Now then, now then, whatever is all this noise about?" said Daddy, giving Katie a good shake to wake her up.

"Oh, is that you, Daddy, really? I'm so glad it's you! Where's Mamma? Is she all right?"

"Of course she is," said Daddy, "she's downstairs cooking my supper."

"I'm so glad," said Katie, "I must go and see her at once. And with that she jumped out of bed, gave Daddy a big hug, kissed Baby Brother all over his dear little face, and ran downstairs to hug Mamma, too.

Then she told them all that had happened and how she really would try hard never to be cross with them any more.

Coals of Fire

"DADDY," cried Donovan, running in from school, "that boy Lionel is the meanest fellow in the school."

"Hallo, hallo, what's the matter now?" said Daddy.

"Oh, he's just terribly mean. He's always calling me names and everything I do he says is bad or stupid and he's always setting the other boys against me with his tales."

"Tut, tut, tut!" said Daddy. "It surely can't be as bad as that."

"Yes, it is," said Donovan. "And what's more, I'm not going to stand it any longer. Big as he is, I'm going to fight him to-morrow."

"Well, that's interesting," said Daddy, smiling. "I hope you will tell me when it's going to come off so I can come along and pick up the pieces."

"There won't be any pieces left of him," said Donovan vehemently.

"What? are you going to swallow him afterwards?"

Donovan laughed.

"Do you know," said Daddy, "I can tell you how to pay that boy back."

"Can you?" cried Donovan, all eagerness. "How?"

"Would you like to put some coals of fire on his head?"

"Anything," said Donovan. "Anything."

69

"Well, I'll get the prescription for you so you can do it."

So Daddy went into his study and brought out a book. After a little searching he found the place.

"Ah, here it is," he said.   "Listen, Donovan: 'If thine enemy hunger, feed him; if he thirst, give him drink: for in so doing thou shalt heap coals of fire on his head.' "   (Rom. 12:20.)

"Aw," said Donovan, "that's no good; I'd rather fight him."

"But," said Daddy, "this is much better. If you fight him you cannot hurt him much; but this way you pour coals of fire on his head. You will burn him all up."

"Splendid!" said Donovan.   "But I don't like that way of doing it."

"Why not try it?" said Daddy.   "It's worth trying, anyway."

"I'll see," said Donovan.   "I'll think it over."

Donovan thought it over and it was not long before something began to happen.

Next morning, on his way to school, who should he meet but the hated Lionel.

"Just my luck," said Lionel, as he came up with Donovan.   "Got up late and missed my breakfast. Suppose you've been eating the fat of the land."

"No breakfast!" said Donovan kindly. "Poor chap! You must be hungry. Do have my lunch right now. Yes, I did have a good breakfast, so you really must have my lunch."

Lionel was "knocked out" more completely than if he had received a blow between the eyes.   He looked first at Donovan and then at the lunch.

"You're kidding me," he said. "You don't mean it."

"Really I do," said Donovan. "Do take it, there's a good chap."

"Awfully decent of you. Thanks," said Lionel, taking the little parcel and beginning to eat. "But you will have a bit yourself, won't you?"

Donovan took a sandwich and they walked on to school together, munching in silence.

"Hot this morning," said Lionel, after they had gone some distance. "Wish I could get a drink somewhere."

"A drink?" said Donovan. "Let me see, where can we get one? I should like one as well."

"Pity we can't get some of that lemonade in that shop over there," said Lionel.

"I've got an idea," said Donovan. "I've got twopence on me. What about it? Let's go over, shall we?"

"Well, I don't want to take your money," said Lionel. "I'll wait till we get to the playground."

"Oh no, come along with me," said Donovan. "We'll have a glass each. Looks good, doesn't it?"

So they went in, bought a glass of lemonade each, and then hurried on to school.

That evening Daddy was waiting at the gate for Donovan.

"Hallo," he said, "how did the fight go? I hope you won."

"I did," said Donovan with a twinkle in his eye. "I just burnt him all up."

"Whatever do you mean?" asked Daddy.

"Why, I did what you said. I fed him with my

lunch and I gave him a drink of lemonade and—well
—he suddenly changed. He's been as different as
could be all day. We've been like old friends all the
time.''

"Splendid! Well done, Donovan!" said Daddy.
"I hope you'll win all your battles just like that."

Tell-Tale Topsy

TOPSY had one big fault. She was for ever telling tales about her sister and brothers.

Just so surely as Mamma went out of the house for a little while, Topsy was there on the doorstep ready for her when she came back with some story or other of the misdeeds of John or Mary or Baby Joe.

Mamma went down the garden on washing day to hang out the clothes. When she got back, sure enough, there was Topsy waiting with a tale.

"Mamma," she began, "Mary's been quarrelling with John while you've been out."

Whereupon Mary rushed up, crying, "No, I haven't, Mamma. We never quarrelled; Topsy's telling fibs again."

Another time Mamma went out shopping. When she returned Topsy was there as usual to tell how Baby Joe had been tugging at the curtains and had pulled one down, how John had been talking crossly to Mary, and how Mary had dropped a saucer and broken it.

Mamma was getting tired of it. "Topsy!" she said one day, "if you don't stop telling tales about others I shall really have to do something to you."

"But you told me to tell you if they hurt themselves."

"Of course," said Mamma. "Always tell me about anything that might do them harm, but that doesn't mean you are to come rushing to me about every little fault. If Mary breaks a saucer it is for

Mary to tell me, and nobody else. Now mind, in future if the wrong person tells me about anything, or if anyone brings me a tale about some petty, trivial thing, I shall fine that one a penny out of his savings box."

That was a terrible threat for Mamma to make, for pennies were scarce and there were very few in the children's savings boxes.

Of course, Topsy soon forgot what Mamma had said, and the very next morning she came running upstairs, crying, "Mamma, Mamma, John's spilled the milk on the table cloth."

"A penny, please," said Mamma.

"A penny?" said Topsy. "What for?"

"Telling tales," said Mamma.

Poor Topsy felt very bad about it, but she had to fetch her savings box, take out a precious penny, and hand it to Mamma. Even so she did not remember long. That same day she came tearing to Mamma with the news that Mary had torn a hole in her pinafore.

"Penny, please," said Mamma.

"What for this time?" asked Topsy.

"Telling tales again," said Mamma.

Topsy found her box again and brought out yet another penny. But, do you know, within ten minutes she came running to Mamma again.

"Mamma, Mamma, Baby Joe has drawn pictures all over Mary's copy-book."

"Penny, please," said Mamma.

"Oh dear!" cried Topsy. "Have I got to keep on giving away my pennies? I soon shan't have any left."

"You can stop just as soon as you like," said Mamma. "Just don't tell me any more tales."

Well, Topsy didn't stop all at once, but when she had paid over to Mamma the very last penny in her box, with many tears she decided that she wouldn't tell tales any more.

A Scene in the Classroom

THERE was quite a storm in the classroom of Lower 4B. Teacher was out and the girls were talking together excitedly.

"It's a shame!" said one.

"It ought not to be allowed," said another.

"My mother says I'm not to speak to her," said Maggie Bee.

"Not to speak to whom?" asked Doreen, coming to see what was the matter.

"To Helen, of course," said Maggie sharply.

"And why not?" asked Doreen.

"Why, don't you know, she's a scholarship girl. I think it's a downright shame letting scholarship girls come into our class."

"If they come in we'll not have anything to do with them," said another.

"We won't play with them," sniggered a third.

"But whyever not?" asked Doreen bravely. "What's the matter with scholarship girls?"

"Of course there's something the matter with them," said Maggie Bee. "My mother ought to know and she told me not to speak to them."

"Well, of all the mean things I've ever heard," said Doreen, "that is the meanest."

"What do you know about it?" chorused the others. "Maggie's mother ought to know better than you."

76

"Well, I know what my mother told me," said Doreen, facing the crowd of girls courageously.

"And what's that, pray?" asked Maggie with a lofty look.

"I'll tell you if you really want to know," said Doreen. "My mother says that scholarship girls are more worthy to be here than we are, for they have studied hard and passed exams and we are here just because our mothers have got money to pay for us. I admire them. It isn't just money that makes people nice."

"Hasn't made you nice, has it?" snapped Maggie.

Some of the girls laughed and Doreen blushed a little.

"I don't mind what you say about me," she said, "but I do mind when you say unkind things about the poor. There is nothing so mean and snobbish as refusing to speak to someone just because she has come here with a scholarship."

"Ha, ha, ha!" laughed Maggie Bee. But it was a hollow laugh, for she knew Doreen was right and that the other girls were being won over to her point of view.

"Well, " said Doreen, turning away. "You can say what you like, Maggie Bee, but I'm going to be friends with Helen, scholarship or no scholarship. She may have cheaper clothes than the rest of us, but she has a good heart, and my mother says that's what matters most."

"Indeed it does," said a familiar voice.

It was teacher. In the heat of the discussion she had crept up unnoticed. All the girls scattered to their places and in a moment were quiet as mice again.

"Doreen's speech," said the teacher, "was the

most beautiful thing I've heard in this classroom. She shall have ten extra marks to-day. If God is no respecter of persons, why should we be?"

Doreen smiled and blushed a little and Maggie hung her head. At the other side of the classroom Helen resolved that as soon as class was over she would give Doreen those two toffees she had been saving to eat on the way home.

Stories for the
Tiny Tots

The Land Where the Tears Get Dry

ONCE upon a time there was a little boy.

He was running round the dining-room just after dinner when he slipped on a piece of mashed potato.

Of course he fell down and started to cry. You should have seen the tears! They rolled down his cheeks like raindrops.

Mamma said he was a bad boy for dropping the piece of mashed potato off his plate, when he should have put it into his mouth, and also for running round the table. This only made the little boy cry all the more.

Just then the door opened and in walked Daddy. He said, "What's all this noise about? All these tears dropping on the floor will make that piece of mashed potato into a dreadful mess."

And the little boy cried more still.

So Daddy, picking him up in his arms, said, "Let us go to the Land where the Tears Get Dry." And they both went off on a long journey—out into the hall, up the stairs, into the bedrooms, down the stairs again, and into Daddy's study. And just as they got there and sat down in Daddy's Big Chair the little boy began to laugh and all the tears dried up!

© P. Phillips, Ipswich

*Mending **Little** Brother's wheelbarrow.*

Teddy and the Tools

TEDDY was sure he was going to be a carpenter when he grew up. He could not see a hammer without wanting to hit something with it. Whenever he could get any nails he liked to hammer them into wood. He did not mind very much what wood it was, so long as it was soft wood. He did not like hard wood, for the nails just bent or fell out.

Teddy liked to mend things, in his own way. Sometimes he would mend them quite well, as when his little brother's wheelbarrow lost a leg and he nailed it on again.

But sometimes he tried to mend things he should have left alone.

Now Daddy had told him that he must not take any more nails nor any more tools out of his shed. Indeed, Daddy had said that if Teddy **did** take any more things out of Daddy's shed it would be a bad job for Teddy.

But Teddy forgot. One day he saw that Mamma had put a chair outside for Daddy to mend. The back was coming off it, and Teddy said to himself, "I can mend that easily. I will give Daddy a surprise when he comes home from the office to-night."

So he took Daddy's hammer again and Daddy's nails and he nailed the back of the chair on again. Then he put the chair back in the dining-room. But he did not notice that he had put in many more nails than were necessary and that one of them had gone right through the wood.

So of course when Daddy came home and sat down on the chair he did get a surprise, for he sat right down on the nail.

And then Teddy got a surprise too, for Daddy said he must learn not to be disobedient any more.

→ → →

Daddy and the Ducks

DADDY had taken his two little girls down to the pond in the park. And there were ducks in the pond, grey ducks, brown ducks, and white ducks.

"Daddy," said Iris as she threw a piece of bread to one of the ducks and watched the bird gobble it up, "Why are ducks?"

"Because," said Daddy, "God made them."

"But why did God make them?" asked Patsy.

"Because—er—" hesitated Daddy, "because God thought He would like to have some ducks."

"Are they good ducks or bad ducks?" asked Iris.

"Very good ducks indeed," said Daddy.

"How do you know?" asked Iris.

"Don't you see," said Daddy, "how they eat all the food that is put before them without grumbling? See, they eat greens and potatoes and bread and never grumble a bit."

"But we are not ducks," said Patsy knowingly.

"No, but you are Daddy's ducky-daddles and you must be just as good as these pretty ducks in the pond."

The Baby a Princess Found

ONCE upon a time there was a little baby, and his mamma put him in a little boat down by the river, in some bulrushes. Then she asked God to send His angels to look after her baby and keep him safely from the wicked king who wanted to kill him.

The next day a pretty princess came down to the river to bathe. She saw the little boat in the bulrushes and she said, "Oh, what a pretty little baby! I must have it for my own."

Just then a little girl ran up and she said, "Please, m'am, would you like me to fetch someone to look after the baby for you?"

And the pretty princess said, "Please do."

So the little girl ran as fast as her legs would carry her all the way home, and she cried, "Mamma, come quick! The princess has found Baby Brother!"

Mamma dropped what she was doing and ran, just as she was, all the way down to the river. And she saw the pretty princess and the other ladies and the bulrushes and the little boat and her darling baby.

And the pretty princess said to the mamma, "Will you look after this baby for me, please?"

And the mamma said, "Indeed, I will." And she hugged her little baby ever so tight and ran back home with him and the little girl as fast as ever they could go. And they all lived happily for a long time afterward.

Watering the garden. © P. Phillips, Ipswich

Winnie's Water Can

WINNIE loved to play with water. Indeed she was always playing with it when her mamma wasn't looking.

One day she asked her mamma if she could water the garden. She asked so nicely that Mamma at last told her she could do so if she promised not to wet her shoes and stockings.

So Winnie went off to find a water can. She could not find her own little water can so she thought she would try to use Daddy's water can. She put it under the garden tap and turned on the water. When she had filled the can half full she found she could not lift it. So she tried to pour some out. Of course it would not go the right way and some went over her shoes.

Winnie did not mind a bit, for she liked to have her shoes wet. So when enough water had run away over the path and over her shoes, she picked up the can and struggled with it over to Mamma's flower bed. She tilted it up, but when she tried to hold it with one hand, as she had seen Daddy do, again the water came over her shoes and stockings. In fact more water went over her shoes and stockings than went on the garden.

Just then Mamma came up and said, "Whatever are you doing with that big can, Winnie?" And Winnie said, "I'm watering your garden, Mamma dear." But Mamma replied, "I'm afraid that is just what you are not doing, Winnie dear. You are just watering your little toes and that's not the way to make them grow."

So poor little Winnie had to go indoors and sit very still until her stockings and shoes got dry again and her feet were warmed by the fire. Then she promised her mamma that she really wouldn't play with water any more.

The Twins' Morning Prayer

Dear Lord,
Thank You for a good night's rest,
And for this new day.
Thank You for this nice home, and food,
*   and clothes.*
Bless me, and make me good and kind
*   to-day.*
Help me to help Mamma all day long.
Bless her in her work at home.
Bless Daddy in his work, too.
Keep us all well and strong,
For Jesus' sake,
*   Amen.*

The Man Who Ran Away from God

ONE day God said to a man, "I want you to go to a big city and preach to the people and make them good."

But the man said to himself, "I don't want to go. The people in that city are unkind and they will hurt me if I tell them to be good. I will run away where God can't find me."

So he got into a big boat and sailed far out to sea. But after a little while a great storm arose, so bad that the sailors thought the boat would surely sink. They said to one another, "There must certainly be a bad man on this boat or God would never send such a storm as this."

They asked this one and that, and finally found the man who was trying to run away from God. He said to them, "I'm so sorry for you all; it's all my fault. Throw me overboard and the storm will stop."

But the sailors were kind men and did not want to throw him overboard, and they tried ever so hard to reach the land.

It was no use; the storm got worse and worse and the boat rocked and tossed and tossed and rocked, until at last the sailors decided to throw the poor man overboard.

So they picked him up by his legs and his arms and cried, "One, Two, Three!——"

Splash! went the poor man as he dropped into the

water and sank down and down and down. How cold it must have felt!

And then what do you suppose happened?

Well, a great big fish came along with his mouth wide open and swallowed him all up. Suddenly the poor man found himself sliding down a hot, dark, greasy passage and go plop! into the fish's inside.

It must have been terrible down there. The poor man must have felt awfully sick and uncomfortable. How he wished he had not tried to run away from God!

He had just enough breath left to pray, so he cried out to God, "Please let me out of this terrible place and I will go at once to the big city and tell the people to be good."

And just then the big fish got a terrible pain in his inside and he brought the poor man up again and landed him safely on the sand by the seashore.

When he felt better, he washed himself, put on some clean clothes, and set out at once for the big city where God had wanted him to go. And no sooner had he preached to the people there than they all wanted to be good at once and nobody wanted to do him any harm after all. What a pity the man didn't go there at first when God spoke to him! And how foolish of him to try to run away from God!

God is always near us, wherever we are. "If I take the wings of the morning, and dwell in the uttermost part of the sea; even there shall Thy hand lead me, and Thy right hand shall hold me." Psa. 139:9, 10.

Mixing in the Love

MAMMA was making the Christmas puddings while Freddie and Jimmie looked on. They liked to watch Mamma make Christmas puddings because she put in such nice things and every now and then she would give them a sultana or a tiny piece of peel.

Mamma said that making the Christmas puddings should be a very happy time, for it was getting ready for the happiest day of the year. She said that everything she put into the pudding meant something good or kind. The big raisins stood for charity, the little currants for kind thoughts, the flour for friendliness, the butter for good-will, the spice for good deeds. Putting in the eggs and milk to bind it all together would be like mixing in the love, Mamma said.

Just as Mamma was in the middle of making the pudding, Mrs. Jones called over the wall to ask a favour.

"I'll have to go in next door for a few minutes," Mamma said to Freddie and Jimmie, "so mind you be good till I come back."

Mamma was away much longer than she expected and Freddie and Jimmie got tired of waiting. They thought they might just as well help Mamma a little.

"I'm going to stir the pudding for Mamma," said Freddie, getting hold of the big spoon. "I know she'll be so glad to find it all stirred up when she gets back."

"Jimmie want to stir it all up too," said his little brother.

"Mixing in the love."

© Topical

So Freddie put Jimmie up on the table and gave him a spoon as well.

Of course, they stirred the pudding all over the place. Some of it went on their cheeks and noses, and now and then some of the nice bits went into their mouths. Finding a cupful of egg-yolks, Freddie put that in too, and he was just trying hard to stir the sticky paste when the back door opened all of a sudden and in ran Mamma.

"Oh, my dears! what are you doing?" she cried.

"Well," said Freddie, quite unconcerned, "we stirred up all the kind thoughts and good deeds and now are just mixing in the love."

And, of course, Mamma couldn't say anything to them after that.

The Twins' Evening Prayer

— ◆ ◆ ◆ —

Dear Lord,
Thank You for a happy day,
And for all the nice things You have
*   given me.*
Bless me now and make me a good boy.
Bless all the poor people,
And the sick people in the hospitals.
Bless the missionaries;
Help them to teach the black boys and
*   girls about Jesus.*
Bless dear, dear Daddy and Mamma.
Keep us all safe.
Give me a good sleep all night
For Jesus' sake,
*   Amen.*

Two beautiful things.

© Topical

Beautiful Things

SOME time ago a competition was held in Australia and a prize offered for the most beautiful child and the most beautiful dog. On the other page you can see those who won the prize. I think they deserved it, don't you?

How we all love to look at beautiful things—and to possess them! Beautiful girls and beautiful boys, beautiful babes and beautiful toys!

Little girls like pretty dresses and nice-looking dolls.

Little boys like bright red motor-cars and smart-looking steam engines.

But have you ever noticed that some things are not always as nice inside as they are outside? There is a very old saying that, "All is not gold that glitters;" and it is very true.

Do you know, one time a boy's daddy gave him a fine-looking steam engine for Christmas and the very first time he wound it up the spring broke. It looked good outside, but it was bad inside. Wasn't the poor little boy disappointed!

And one time a mamma gave a little girl a most beautiful-looking doll. She was so pleased. But what do you suppose happened? Why, just as the little girl was hugging the doll and kissing its pretty face, its eyes fell in! And then it looked so ugly that the little girl felt she could never love it any more.

If you notice, you will find many things that look

nice outside but are poor and cheap and worthless inside.

Sometimes it happens this way with little boys and girls. Perhaps Mamma will dress her children in nice new clothes so that they look so clean and spotless that one would think they were almost little angels dropped down from the skies. But all of a sudden something goes wrong. They begin to quarrel and there is such a noise and a squabbling that one would think that they were not children at all but a lot of little monkeys from Africa.

It isn't just clothes and "looks" that make people beautiful. There are lots of little girls with the most lovely curly hair who can be as cross as a bear when they can't have their own way.

And there's many a little boy looking very smart in a new suit of clothes who can be as stubborn as a mule when he chooses.

Have you ever read the story of David? Well, when God was looking for someone to make king of Israel many fine-looking young men presented themselves. They were tall and strong, and some of them, perhaps, well dressed. But God was not satisfied. He told His prophet Samuel to send for the brave, honest little shepherd boy who was out in the fields keeping his father's sheep. He had a beautiful face, so the Bible tells us, and he was beautiful inside too. He had a good heart.

And God said to Samuel, "Arise, anoint him: for this is he. For the Lord seeth not as man seeth; for man looketh on the outward appearance, but the Lord looketh on the heart." 1 Sam. 16:7, 12.

So David was made king of Israel because he was good inside as well as outside.

It is goodness, not fine clothes, that makes people beautiful. The plainest-looking folk are often the most loved because of their good hearts.

It is goodness, not outward beauty, that God looks for first. We cannot hide our crossness from God by putting on our Sabbath clothes. Nor will a kind heart pass His notice because it is clothed in rags.

And when Jesus comes back to this earth again— as He is coming very soon—to take His children to the wonderful home He is preparing for them, He will not bother much about their looks, you may be sure, What He will ask is, Does this child love Me? Is he a good boy? Has this little girl a loving heart?

If they do not love Him, He will just leave them behind. He simply couldn't take them into His beautiful kingdom and let them spoil it for everybody else. That is why the Bible says that when Jesus comes again, "The Son of man shall send forth His angels, and they shall gather out of His kingdom all things that offend, and them which do iniquity; and shall cast them into a furnace of fire." Matt. 13:41.

We don't like to read about that; it doesn't sound nice. But then, we do not need to have that happen to us. Jesus wants to have us all in His beautiful home, and He has done everything to make it possible. All He asks is that we love Him and try to be good as He was when He was a little child. Then when He comes we shall hear Him say to us:

"Come, you whom My Father has blessed, come into your inheritance in the realm prepared for you from the foundation of the world. For I was hungry, and you fed Me, I was thirsty and you gave Me drink, I was a stranger and you entertained Me, I was un-clothed and you clothed Me, I was in prison and you visited Me. Then the just will answer, 'Lord, when did we see You hungry and fed You? Or thirsty and gave You drink? When did we see You a stranger and entertain You? Or unclothed and clothed You?' The King shall answer them, 'I tell you truly, in so far as you did it to one of these brothers of Mine, even to the least of them, you did it to Me.' " Matt. 25: 34-40 (Moffat's translation).

That is God's idea of goodness. That is the beauty He loves. Those are the beautiful things He wants us to do. Those who do them He will take to the beautiful land where all is peace and joy and happiness, and where cross and ugly things never enter.

Let's plan to be there, shall we?—and be ready when Jesus comes.

Note.—The Companion Volumes to this book, "Bedtime Stories" (First, Second, Third, Fourth, Fifth, Seventh, and Eighth Series), can be obtained at 1/- each, or any five numbers for 4/- from the printers and publishers:

The Stanborough Press Ltd., Watford, Herts.

Printed and published in Great Britain by The Stanborough Press Ltd., Watford.
5M/394/1132

UNCLE ARTHUR'S
BEDTIME STORIES
(SEVENTH SERIES)

With Every Good Wish

To ....

From ....

By Shields   *Jesus as a boy at Nazareth.* © Autotype Fine Art Co.

Uncle Arthur's
BEDTIME STORIES
(Seventh Series)

By ARTHUR S. MAXWELL

Editor of "Present Truth," author of
"Great Issues of the Age," "Protestantism
Imperilled!" "Christ's Glorious Return,"
"After Many Days," etc.

"Train up a child in the way he should go:
and when he is old, he will not depart from
it." Proverbs 22:6.

Registered at Stationers' Hall by

THE STANBOROUGH PRESS LTD.,
WATFORD, HERTS.

CONTENTS

PREFACE

AND so the years roll on! Here, as much to our surprise as anybody's, is the seventh series.

As for the rest, they have gone to the four corners of the earth, two millions of them, we are told, being broadcast also from many stations. And in reply, from the ends of the earth, come kindly words of appreciation. Unknown friends spring up everywhere to greet us. We are grateful.

And now we send number seven on its mission. All the stories, as before, are based on fact, and true to life. All are planned to teach some virtue or frown upon some sin. All are loyal to the Bible, exalting the commandments of God and the teachings of Jesus. That they may be a blessing to all who read them, and lead many a child into ways of righteousness and truth, is the sincere desire of

THE AUTHOR.

Copyright 1930.
The Stanborough Press Ltd.,
Watford, Herts.

Dragging the sledges down the village street.   Ⓒ **Topical**

A Change of Plan

A Christmas Story

THE wireless weather report said that snow was coming. This was good news for Joe and Gerald. It set them ablaze with energy.

They had often talked about making sledges for themselves, but so far had never done so. The good news about the snow made them decide to make one each. And with a right good will they began the task.

Every moment they could spare from their school work the boys spent in the shed at the bottom of Gerald's garden, sawing, planing, hammering, until at last, to their great joy, the sledges were completed and ready for the arrival of the snow.

But it did not come. Probably the clouds were blown away after the weather experts had looked at them. However that may be, it is certain that for many days there were two sledges in Gerald's garden with nothing to slide them on.

The school term ended and still there was no snow. Day after day went by, cold and wet. There seemed about as much prospect of snow as of a heat wave. The boys gave up hope and wished they had never taken the trouble to make their sledges.

At last Christmas eve arrived and with it came a sudden change. The rain stopped, the thermometer went down with a rush, and a strong wind arose.

"Something is going to happen," said Joe, as he went to bed that night. And he was right.

In the morning the clouds had gone and the rising sun glistened on a vast expanse of snow. A heavy fall had covered the whole landscape with a glorious white mantle.

Gerald was overjoyed. As soon as he awoke he guessed what had happened, for he could see the reflection of the snow on the ceiling. He leaped out of bed, dressed as quickly as he could, and rushed down the garden to the shed where the precious sledges had been stored so long. With difficulty he hauled them both over the snow up to the house, and then ran off to find Joe.

How happy they were! This was better than their highest expectations. No Christmas day could have started so joyously for them. They decided that they would go off at once to a neighbouring hill and enjoy themselves to the full.

They trotted off down the street, dragging their sledges behind them. School friends shouted to them.

"Lucky fellows," they cried, "let's have a ride."

"No fear," cried Joe and Gerald, "we're going off by ourselves to-day."

"Lend us one of your sledges," cried another.

"Oh, rather!" shouted Joe. "You should have made one for yourself."

Ralph Morton, the lame boy, waved his hand cheerfully from his window and wished them a jolly time.

"Decent of him, wasn't it?" said Gerald.

"Yes," said Joe, "'specially as he can never hope to pilot a sledge of his own."

Just then they passed Madge Green's house. They had always been friendly with her and her little sisters. She greeted them cheerfully as usual and wished them a happy Christmas.

"Wish I could come for a slide," she said, "but I can't to-day. I'm helping Mother all I can so that she may have a really happy Christmas."

The boys passed on. Soon they were out of the town and ascending the hill, dragging their sledges behind them. Then they prepared their slide and the fun began.

Swish! Away they went down the hill. Then up to the top again. Then another glorious slide. So they played together for a couple of hours.

After awhile, however, Joe noticed a change coming over Gerald's face.

A game of snowballs.   © Topical

"What's up, old chap?" asked Joe with some concern, as they climbed up the hill together.

"Nothing much," said Gerald, "only somehow I'm not getting as much fun out of this as I thought I should."

"Aren't you?" said Joe. "I'm not, either. Of course, it's jolly nice in a way, yet I don't sort of feel comfortable. I wonder why it is?"

"Funny we should both feel the same way," said Gerald, "isn't it?"

"Awfully funny," said Joe, as they trudged on up to the top.

Swish! Down they went again.

On the way up they discussed their strange feelings again.

"I think I know what is the matter," said Joe.

"What?" asked Gerald.

"I keep thinking about Ralph."

"So do I," said Gerald. "And Madge and the others. I wish we hadn't left them behind. Bit mean of us, wasn't it?"

"Yes," said Joe.

There was silence again as they climbed slowly upwards.

"I think we'll only have one more," said Joe.

"All right," said Gerald.

They had the last slide and then turned towards home. On the way they talked of how they would spend the afternoon. As they reached the town they began calling at the homes of some of their little friends who had no sledges. What they said seemed to make them very happy.

Dinner was scarcely over when there was a loud knock at their front door. Running out, Joe and

Gerald found a happy, excited group of children waiting for them.

"Hurrah!" they all cried when they saw the two boys. "I'll be first," said one, and "Me, me, me first!" called another.

Then, sorting the visitors out, Joe and Gerald put two or three of them on each of their sledges and began to give them rides up and down the street. Oh, the shrieks of joy! How they all did laugh and yell!

All the afternoon they kept it up—except for a game of snowballs now and then—giving rides to all the children in turn, until at last, too weary to run any more, Joe and Gerald sent them all home and put the hard-worked sledges back in the shed once more.

"Well, it's been a glorious day," said Gerald, "but the afternoon was the best of all."

"Rather," said Joe, "what a great time it was! The morning on the hill wasn't anything like it."

"Do you know, Joe," said Gerald, "I had made up my mind that I never would let anyone use my sledge, but I didn't really begin to enjoy it until I started to share it with the others."

"You're right," said Joe. "Doesn't the Bible say somewhere that 'It is more blessed to give than to receive'? I think that's why we both felt so much happier after dinner, don't you?"

And Gerald agreed. "This is the best Christmas day we've had," he said.

Launching the lifeboat.   Ⓒ Topical

A Cry in the Night

NOWADAYS we are all familiar with wireless and loud-speakers, batteries and head-phones, and all sorts of strange things that nobody had heard of a few years ago. Almost every home has its crystal set or its valve set. And what a wonderful thing it is that these little instruments can bring the sound of people's voices to us from hundreds of miles away!

Most of the programmes we listen to come from big broadcasting stations situated in various parts of the country, but occasionally one can hear messages from ships at sea or even from aeroplanes in flight. The tic-tic-tic that one sometimes hears is probably one ship talking to another in Morse code. People who understand this code can therefore learn what one captain is saying to another.

Some time ago there was a man in the south of England who made it his hobby to listen to these messages from ships. Long after the big broadcasting stations had closed down for the night he would go on listening, picking up one ship after another.

Then one stormy night his aerial was blown down. He might have left it down and gone to bed. But no, he was so enthusiastic about his hobby that he went out in the dark, climbed the fir tree at the end of his garden, fixed up the wire as best he could, and went back to his set again.

Hardly had he begun to tune in than he became

13

aware of the persistent call of S.O.S., the universal
signal of a ship in distress. This, he thought, was
interesting indeed, and well worth the trouble he had
taken to fix his aerial. The call continued, S.O.S.—
S.O.S.—S.O.S.

Suddenly it dawned upon him that the call was not
being answered. Of course, he told himself, that was
why it was being repeated so continuously. Could it
be, then, that he was the only one listening to this cry
for help?

Just then, in broken English, came this urgent
and piteous appeal:

"Please everybody come and help."

The man jumped to his feet and ran to the tele-

Wireless operator listening-in on board ship.   ⓒ Topical

phone. Ringing up the nearest radio station he asked
if they had heard the call. They had not. He begged
them to listen. They agreed. Messages were sent
out asking other ships to stop signalling for a time.
At once the cry of the little ship was heard. Immediately help was sent and the ship was saved.

An hour after telephoning to the radio station the
man's aerial was blown down again. It had stayed
up just long enough for the signal of distress to be
heard!

Strange, wasn't it? Surely the hand of God was
in this thing for some good purpose.

And just as this lonely man with his little home-
made set was able to bring help to that storm-tossed
ship, while the big station was too busy to hear its cry,
so even little children, small though they be, may hear
many a cry in the night from sad and suffering souls
and, by kind and loving deeds, bring help and blessing to many such ships in distress.

A jolly time by the sea.

© Topical

The Storm

KEN should have been a very happy boy. Was he not at the seaside for a glorious fortnight's holiday? Did he not have a new bucket and spade? Had not Daddy given him a new boat with red sails? Did he not have beautiful sands to play on and the cool, refreshing sea in which to bathe?

He did—but he was not happy.

He had just had a very good dinner, too, but still he was not happy. In fact, he was feeling very rebellious, and he looked it. An ugly scowl covered his face and his lips pouted out quite half an inch.

Of course it was all about nothing, as usual. Daddy had asked him to stop throwing stones as it was annoying other people on the beach. Ken thought he should be allowed to throw stones on the beach, and Daddy had to interfere quite strenuously before his little son would stop. Hence that terrible look on Ken's face.

"Come and help us build a big castle," said Daddy, trying to make things easy for him. "The tide will soon be up, and we can watch it attack our fortress."

"Don't want to build any old castle," said Ken.

"Come along, come along," said Daddy.

"Don't want to," said Ken, fiercely, turning round and walking away.

"All right," said Daddy, "I'll build it myself."

And so saying he picked up a spade and began to dig.

Meanwhile Ken trudged on and on along the beach. Really it was a very funny sight, for he was only a little boy of nine, and there he was with his hands deep in his pockets, and his brow all puckered up as though he were plotting a revolution. Farther and farther he wandered. He did not seem to notice the passing of time, nor the fact that he had left his family and friends far behind.

Still boiling with anger he trudged savagely on. He didn't want to play with the others any more. He didn't want to be with anybody, he told himself. He wanted to be by himself and do just as he pleased. Now he could throw stones where he liked and when he liked, for there wasn't anybody anywhere. And he was glad, glad, glad about it, that he was!

Just then a sudden chilling of the air made him look upwards. Till now the sun had been shining brilliantly. The past few days, indeed, had been fine and hot. But now a dark cloud obscured the sun and a cold gust of wind came from the south-west.

Ken slowed down a little. He did not like the look of the sky. But turn back? No, indeed, he wouldn't.

Ten minutes later Ken looked at the sky again Almost all the blue had gone. Rising fast from the horizon were black, angry-looking clouds. The occasional gusts of wind had become a gale. The sea that had been so calm and still a little while before was being lashed to fury.

A dull boom in the distance brought Ken to a standstill. His little face lost its scowl and turned very pale. He didn't like storms.

Boom, boom, boom! rolled the thunder, getting louder and louder.

Flash! Across the black clouds leapt lightning more terrible than Ken had ever seen.

Crack! Boom! Crash! A terrific peal of thunder sounded right above him.

Ken stood still, petrified with fright. Wildly he looked around for shelter, but there was none. Along that lonely beach not even a seagull could have found cover.

And now the rain!

Swish! Swish! Swish! Driven hard by the gale it beat upon the beach and splashed with an uncanny hissing into the sea.

Poor Ken was soaked in a moment. Water streamed through his shirt. He dropped beside a breakwater and buried his head in his hands.

Boom! Boom! rolled the thunder, as loud and terrible as before.

"Oh dear!" cried Ken to himself, "why did I come so far away? I wish I had stopped with the others. Oh dear! Will this thunder never stop?"

Crash! Another terrifying peal thundered over his head. It was too much for the little chap. Tears flowed at last, rolling down his cheeks and mingling with the rain that was pouring in torrents over him.

Ah, what was that? Another sound had reached his ears amid the storm.

Surely that was a footstep. Someone was walking on the beach somewhere.

Ken looked up and peered over the breakwater through the blinding rain.

Hurrah! Yes! Someone with an umbrella held

close and low before him as he fought his way against the gale.

Ken felt he had never been so glad to see somebody before. He called out, but his little voice was drowned by the storm.

Crack! A flash and a report right overhead again sent Ken huddling beside his breakwater.

But the footsteps drew nearer. Ken peeped over again. Yes, there was the umbrella, much nearer now.

Then another fear gripped his heart. Would this person care for him? Would he want to stop in this storm? Would he want to share his umbrella in such rain as this? Ken huddled down again in fear and discouragement.

The footsteps stopped. Ken looked up. The umbrella was overhead.

"Hallo, Ken," said a familiar voice, "what on earth are you doing here?"

"Oh Dad! Did you come for me?" cried Ken, tears breaking out afresh as he threw his arms round Daddy. "Oh, I'm so glad you've come. I'm sorry I was so mean. I won't be so horrid any more."

"That's all right, son," said Daddy. "We'll forget about all that. But if you ever do want to go walking on your own again I hope you won't choose a day like this."

And then, with the gale behind them and the thunder gradually rolling away into the distance, they walked back hand in hand together.

The Burglar

MURIEL came bounding in from school.

"Oh, Mamma," she cried, "what do you think? Why, almost all the girls in my form are going to Jenny's party on Thursday night."

"Are they?" said Mamma, trying hard to be interested, though she was feeling very tired. "That will be nice."

"But that's not all," said Muriel, "they've almost all told me that they are going to have the loveliest new dresses—silk and crêpe-de-chine, you know, and things like that."

"They must be happy, then," said Mamma.

"Yes, but, Mamma, what about me? I can't go in my old dress."

"It's not very old," said Mamma. "Why, you only had it new for your birthday. Anyhow, dear, I don't think I could possibly finish the other by Thursday."

Muriel did not notice the look of utter weariness that passed over Mamma's face at the very thought of taking on another job just now.

"Mamma!" she cried, very agitated, "you don't mean to say that I shall not have my new dress for Thursday? Why, I've got to have it. I must have it. I couldn't go to Jenny's party without it. Whatever would they think of me? All the other girls with

new frocks on and me in that old cotton thing! Of
course I must have it."

The bright, happy look that was on Muriel's face as
she had bounded into the dining-room had faded away.
In its place was an ugly scowl. And the more she
thought about her fancied grievance, the darker the
scowl became. Gradually she worked herself up into
a thoroughly bad temper.

"I must have my new frock," she cried, stamping
her foot on the floor.

"Now, come," said Mamma, sternly. "It is not
becoming for a little girl to behave like this. I don't
think you would do it if Jenny were here."

"I wouldn't care if anybody were here," cried
Muriel wildly, tears running down her cheeks.

"Now, Muriel," said Mamma, "this is very foolish
of you. You must be over-tired. Please go to your
bedroom. I will bring you your tea later."

Muriel stormed out of the room and up the stairs.
Some time later Mamma went up with a very plain
tea. She did not say much, only stopping long enough
to put little Jimmie to bed. Jimmie did not bother
his head about the state of affairs, though he thought
it was strange that Muriel should go to bed so early.

An hour passed. Muriel tried to sleep, but could
not. Conscience was keeping her awake. She knew
she should be sorry for her very naughty conduct, but
something kept her from saying so. She rolled and
tossed upon her bed. Another hour passed; then
another. At last she dropped into a troubled sleep.

It seemed hardly a moment before she was
awakened by a small hand tugging at her nose. It
was Jimmie.

"Sis, Sis," he was saying, "I'm frightened, let me come into your bed."

Muriel sat up.

"What's the matter, Jimmie?" she said, lifting the shivering little chap in beside her.

"Oh, didn't you hear it? The noise—downstairs!"

"No," said Muriel. "I was asleep. What sort of noise?"

"Someone walking about," said Jimmie.

Muriel listened. It was a dark night, and very still. A cool breeze came in from the wide open window.

Then the clock in the dining-room struck. One —two.

"Why, it's two o'clock," said Muriel. "There can't be anybody about now."

"But there was, just a little while ago," said Jimmie. "You should have heard."

Suddenly Muriel's heart stood still and she seemed to tingle all over. She had heard a footstep in the room beneath her.

"Did you hear it then?" said Jimmie.

"Yes," said Muriel. "I wonder——"

"Do you think it's a burglar?" asked Jimmie in a whisper.

"It might be," said Muriel, now very frightened herself.

"What shall we do?" asked Jimmie. "Do you think he will hurt us?"

Muriel did not know what to say. Her first thought was to dive under the bedclothes. Then she remembered how she had once told the girls at school what

she would do if burglars ever came to her house.
She thought a moment.

"There it is again!" whispered Jimmie, pressing
closer to his big sister.

"Jimmie," said Muriel, "do you know, I'd really
like to see a burglar, just once, so I could tell the girls
at school."

"Would you? I wouldn't," said Jimmie.

"Will you come with me if I go down?" asked
Muriel. "I'll look after you."

Jimmie was doubtful, but at last decided to go.
Together they slipped out of bed. Ever so quietly
they crept to the door and opened it.

Creak! went the hinges, so loud that the two
nearly ran back to bed. But they held each other's
hands a little more tightly and went towards the stairs.

Creak! went the top stair.

They waited a moment and then went down a
little farther.

Creak! went the fifth stair.

Again they waited. Then on farther.

Creak! creak! went the landing.

"He'll hear us," whispered Jimmie. "Let's go
back."

"Wait a minute," whispered Muriel, pressing his
little hand. "We're nearly there. See, there's a
light under the dining-room door. I must see what
a burglar's like and I may never have the chance
again."

"But won't he hurt us?" asked Jimmie.

"We'll run too fast," said Muriel.

They were down in the hall now.

Slowly and ever so quietly they moved towards the

door. It was slightly ajar. Muriel pushed it just a teeny-weeny bit. Then a teeny-weeny bit more. And ever such a teeny-weeny bit more. So it was opened, wider and wider, until at last Muriel thought she could put her head round just enough to see inside.

Jimmie held her hand very tightly as she peered round the corner. And what do you suppose she saw?

"Muriel!" cried a voice, while a pair of scissors clattered on the floor.

"Mamma!" cried Muriel.

They looked at each other.

"Mamma! what are you doing here at this time of the night? It's nearly half-past two and you look worn out."

"Just a little dressmaking," said Mamma.

"Not my dress, surely," cried Muriel. "Oh, it is! Mamma, you shouldn't. I didn't deserve it. You shouldn't have stopped up so long. You were so tired."

She threw her arms round Mamma's neck. "I'm so, so sorry," she said, her tears falling fast.

"Never mind," said Mamma. "The frock is nearly done now. Let us all go to bed. But whatever is Jimmie doing down here?"

"Muriel said I should see a burglar if I came downstairs, and now there isn't one," muttered Jimmie, looking mournful and disappointed.

"I'm sorry," said Muriel, as they went upstairs together, "but Mamma is surely better than a burglar, isn't she?"

"S'pose so," said Jimmie, with a tired little smile.

And so, mother-love, for ever patient, long-suffering, and forgiving, triumphed again.

© Topical

H.M.S. "Victory" flying Nelson's famous signal—"England expects every man to do his duty."

Man Overboard!

MANY a stirring story has been told of the great Lord Nelson, who led the British fleet to many a gallant victory in days of old. You have all read of Trafalgar. Perhaps you have been fortunate enough to see Nelson's flagship in Portsmouth harbour. But here is a story about him that for courage and self-sacrifice outshines perhaps his greatest triumphs.

He was sailing through the Straits of Gibraltar in a small frigate, intent on rejoining the main British fleet stationed some distance out in the Atlantic. Suddenly he was sighted by two Spanish men-of-war. As Spain was at war with Britain, these two ships immediately gave chase to Nelson, hoping to cut him off and destroy his ship before he could reach his fleet.

Nelson, seeing his perilous situation, crowded on all possible sail, hoping against hope that he would come in sight of the fleet before he should be overtaken.

Hour after hour the chase continued, the larger and more powerful Spanish men-of-war slowly but surely overhauling the British ship. Nearer and still nearer they approached. Nelson prepared for action, though he knew the odds were all against him. He would do his best anyhow, and certainly, whatever happened, he would never haul down his flag.

Then suddenly the cry was raised, "Man overboard!" Someone had been struck by a heavy sea and swept over the ship's side.

In those bad old days life was cheap. And in a desperate situation like this, with the enemy drawing nearer every moment, and death staring all in the face, who would care that one poor seaman was lost?

The news was carried to Nelson's ears.

"Man overboard, sir," reported an officer.

"Who is it?" asked Nelson.

"Harvey, sir."

"Harvey! We can't afford to lose Harvey!" cried Nelson.

Then, without a moment's hesitation, he gave that heroic command:

"About sail! Lower a boat."

The men stared at him in amazement, but in those days to hear was to obey. Instantly the word was passed through the ship that Harvey was to be rescued at all costs. A boat was lowered and brave men rowed back seemingly into the very jaws of death to rescue the sinking man.

They saved him.

And then a strange thing happened. Suddenly the Spanish ships were seen to alter their course. With a swift movement they turned and fled in the direction whence they had come. They thought, so it was learned afterwards, that Nelson must surely have sighted the British fleet or he never would have turned at such a moment.

So Nelson's self-sacrifice in that desperate moment saved both himself and all his men.

And it often happens so.

Boisterous Bimbo

IT was half-past four.

All was quiet and peaceful in the Cooper household. Connie, already home from school, had seated herself comfortably in a chair by the fire and started to do her homework. Baby Sister was on the hearth-rug building a castle with her bricks and humming softly to herself.

Suddenly they looked up. They had heard a familiar and unwelcome sound.

"La-la-la-la-la-la-la—"

"Bimbo!" said Connie. "Now there will be no more peace."

She was right.

A moment later the back door was opened violently and banged against the kitchen wall.

"Hallo, hallo!" cried eight-year-old Bimbo. "Where's everybody? La-la-la-la-la-la—"

He burst into the dining-room, flinging the door back against the sideboard with such a crash that a small vase clattered on to the floor and smashed.

"Bimbo, you naughty boy!" cried Connie, "What will Mamma say?"

"Hallo, Con. I couldn't help it. What are you doing there anyway? You don't want to read any more to-day, do you? Come and play conkers."

With that Bimbo emptied his pockets on the table,

conkers by the dozen dropping on the floor and rolling all over the place.

"I don't want to play conkers this evening," said Connie. "I've got to learn this poetry for to-morrow morning."

"Aw, come on," cried Bimbo, "drop that. You can do it later." And so saying he knocked Connie's book out of her hand.

Connie jumped out of her chair in anger.

"What do you mean by that?" she cried. "Why can't you leave people alone?"

"Oh, hoity-toity," teased Bimbo, pulling Connie's hair and kicking her book across the room. Unfortunately it hit Baby Sister's castle and brought it tumbling down in ruins.

"Boo-hoo-hoo!" cried Baby Sister. "You horrid Bimbo! You've broken my castle and I wanted Mamma to see it. Boo-hoo-hoo!"

Then with all the desperation of disappointment she picked up a brick and hurled it with all her baby might at Bimbo's head. He ducked, and it struck a picture on the wall, shattering the glass to fragments.

Just at this moment the back door opened again and in walked Mamma.

"Whatever does all this mean?" she asked, looking round at the angry, tearful faces and the litter of broken glass and china on the floor. "I heard the noise when I was half-way up the garden. Why, the room looks like a battlefield!"

"Wasn't my fault," said Bimbo; "they just don't seem to like me coming home, that's what it is."

"Mamma, it was all his fault," said Connie, heatedly. "We were both so peaceful and happy till he came in. I wish he would never come home from school again."

"And he knocked my lovely castle over," added Baby Sister. "Horrid Bimbo!"

Mamma understood. "You come with me, Bimbo," she said. "I think we must have a little talk together about this."

Bimbo followed Mamma upstairs. While Bimbo took off some of his clothes Mamma found a little strap that she kept for such occasions in her room. Then Bimbo began to sing "La-la-la-la-la—" in a different key.

Afterwards Mamma began to talk with him.

"Bimbo," she said, "you must pull yourself together and behave more like a civilized little boy. You are so wild and rowdy that one would think you belonged to a tribe of savages. Every day you seem to get worse. You are always upsetting the others and making yourself a perfect nuisance."

"I didn't mean to," said Bimbo.

"Of course you didn't," said Mamma, "but if you would only think about it and determine to be different, you would be. And you must. Things cannot go on like this. Why, it's terrible that Connie and Baby should dread the very thought of your coming into the house!"

"Oh dear!" sighed Bimbo.

"I've got an idea," said Mamma. "I want you to make up your mind that directly you come into the house every evening you will say something nice and kind to everybody and think how you can help make the others happy."

"Ugh!" sighed Bimbo.

"You will, won't you?" urged Mamma.

"I'll think about it," said Bimbo.

And at that Mamma left him to do so.

Bimbo did think about it. Indeed, he thought a lot about it. But school came the next day, and he forgot about it. At least, he forgot until he turned the corner of his street on the way home. Then he remembered; and all the way up the street he laid his plans as to what he would do when he got indoors.

Creeping up to the back door he entered so quietly that nobody heard him. Tip-toeing across the room he surprised Connie almost out of her wits by dangling a bag of sweets under her nose.

"I didn't eat all my sweets to-day," he said, "and I brought these home for you and Baby."

"Well, I never!" gasped Connie, too taken aback to know what else to say.

Bimbo, a little self-conscious, ran quickly out into the kitchen again, shut the door softly, and seeing some dirty dishes in the sink, commenced to wash them.

He was in the middle of drying them when Mamma came in.

"Well!" she cried, flopping down upon the nearest chair and holding her hands in the air. "Did you ever! My wild, boisterous Bimbo is tame at last!"

Bimbo heard—and smiled, and always after that, directly he turned the corner of his street on his way home from school he would begin to plan some pleasant surprise to spring on the others.

Soon, instead of Connie and Baby saying, "Oh dear, there's Bimbo coming!" they began to say, "Hurrah! Bimbo will soon be home!"

Rosalind's Medicine

PEOPLE who live in hot countries have to take great care of their health. If they don't, they usually catch some serious disease which causes them great pain and discomfort, and sometimes death.

One of these diseases is malaria. Even the most careful people sometimes get it, but it has been found that if one takes a medicine called quinine the attacks are much less severe.

Now quinine is not a very nice medicine. It has a very bitter taste and most children have a strong dislike for it.

Anyhow, Rosalind certainly had. She hated it, and did not hesitate to tell her mother so.

She lived on a mission station in Africa and malaria was very prevalent in the district. The whole family suffered from it a good deal, Rosalind included.

One day she felt another attack coming on. Mother noticed it, put her to bed, and went for the quinine.

But Rosalind did not want the quinine. She disliked it so much she thought she would rather have the malaria than take the horrid stuff.

Mother begged and implored her to take it but in vain. You know the scene that so often takes place when a little girl is asked to take some nasty medicine! Well, that is just what happened then. Rosalind was obstinate. She would not take the quinine. Mother, knowing that the little girl's life depended on her taking it, began to insist.

"You must take it, Rosalind," she said.

"I don't want to," said the little girl. "It's horrible stuff."

"But you will be very ill indeed if you do not take it," said Mother.

"Then I'll be ill," said Rosalind, defiantly.

"Well," said Mother sternly, "you must take it. I do not want you to be ill. There is too much to do here already, without having a sick child to care for."

"I'll tell you what," said Rosalind. "If you will leave the medicine on the table, and go out of the room, I promise you it will all be gone when you come back."

"All right," said Mother happily, glad for some way out of the struggle. "There it is now. Drink it all up, there's a good girl, and when I come back I will bring you something nice."

Mother went out and closed the door. A little later she returned, saw the glass was empty, and handed Rosalind a sweet. She thought Rosalind did not look very happy, but put it down to the nasty taste of the medicine.

That night Rosalind's temperature went up ever so high and she became delirious.

Mother grew alarmed. Poor Rosalind became steadily worse. Very sick, and racked with pain, she almost wished she could die.

Every moment she could spare, Mother sat by the little girl's bedside to soothe and comfort her.

"Mother," said Rosalind the next evening, "there's something I've got to tell you."

"Is there?" said Mother, "I wonder what it is? But there, perhaps you had better not talk much now. When you get better you can tell me."

"No, I must tell you in case—in case—I don't get better," said Rosalind.

"Whatever can it be then?" asked Mother.

"Well, Mother dear," said Rosalind, "I know why I am so ill."

"Do you, dear?"

"Yes, Mother. You know that medicine I wouldn't take?"

"Yes, I remember," said Mother with a smile. "You mean the medicine you wouldn't take till I went out of the room?"

"Yes," said Rosalind, very sadly, and talking with difficulty. "I never took it."

"Rosalind!"

"Yes, I threw it out of the window."

There was silence for several minutes.

"Are you very cross, Mother," asked Rosalind, after a little while.

"Not cross, only sorry," said Mother.

"Oh, that's much worse," said Rosalind.

"But you understand now, dear, don't you?" said Mother.

"I do, indeed."

"It costs too much, doesn't it, dear, to disobey?"

"It does," said Rosalind.

And they squeezed hands in the gathering darkness while Rosalind resolved that if Jesus would make her well again she would try to be a better girl and never deceive her mother again.

She kept her promise.

Two sweet young things.

© Topical

"A Little Child Shall Lead Them"

YOU may think this is a made-up story, but it isn't. It is absolutely true. I know the little boy and girl it concerns very well indeed and it was their own mamma who told it to me.

Of course the names are not real. I couldn't tell you the real names, could I? So I will call the boy Donald and the girl Margaret. Margaret was five and Donald eight and a half.

It so happened that one day when Mamma was clearing up the dining-room she threw an old Christmas card on to the fire. It was a very old one that had been sent to Margaret at least four years before.

Hardly was it alight, however, than Margaret, spying it, began to make the biggest fuss you ever heard.

"That's my Christmas card," she cried. "You shouldn't have burnt it. I've kept it all this time and I want it. It's mine."

"But it was such a dirty card," said Mamma, trying to make the matter right. "And it has been lying about the place for such a long time I thought you did not want it any more."

"But of course I wanted it," cried Margaret, getting more angry. "You should have known

I wanted it. Why should you burn my things, anyway?"

Mamma tried calmly to explain to Margaret that she had lots of other cards, that all together they were of no real value, and that very soon there would be another Christmas when she would probably receive many more.

But Margaret refused to be reasoned with and began calling her Mamma some very naughty names. Whereupon Mamma tried another method of helping her little daughter—and the neighbours must have wondered what was happening next door. Just what happened I will leave you to guess, but I can tell you that very shortly afterwards a sobbing little girl was getting in between a pair of sheets upstairs.

Donald was in bed by now also, and when Mamma had kissed them both good-night and gone out of the room, he began to talk. Mamma, on the stairs, over-heard what was said.

"Margaret," said Donald, "you must be a good girl, and go fast asleep."

"I can't go to sleep," said Margaret. "I've been so naughty, and I don't want Mamma to whip me any more."

"Yes, dearie," said Donald, with sympathy and wisdom beyond his years, "you have been very naughty, and it made me feel so sad and ill inside, but if you would just say a little prayer all for yourself it would make everything all right."

"I don't know what to say," said Margaret, amid sobs.

"If you like, Margaret, I will help you," said

Donald, "and you could say it after me. Shall I?"
"Yes, please."

There was a pause. Then Donald began.

"Dear Lord Jesus. Now Margaret, do please."

"Dear Lord Jesus," repeated Margaret.

"Help me not to be naughty," said Donald.

"Help me not to be naughty," repeated Margaret.

"Forgive me for showing a naughty temper
to-night," said Donald.

The sobs increased, and Margeret did not speak.

"But you must say it," Donald insisted.

At last Margaret repeated, "Forgive me for showing a naughty temper to-night."

"And make me a good little girlie," continued
Donald.

"And make me a good little girlie," repeated Margaret.

"And please wash all my sins away, for Jesus
Christ's sake, amen," said Donald.

Margaret again repeated after him.

"Is that all now, Donald?" she asked. "And is it
all right?"

"Yes, dear," said Donald, "don't cry any more
now. You know, the sheet you've spoilt in your book
in heaven—where the angels write all that we do—has
now been smudged all over with something like red,
ever so red, crayon and it has hidden up all the nasty
writing about all your naughty tricks and no one can
ever read about them again. That's just what Jesus
does when we are sorry and ask Him to forgive us.
Aren't you pleased, Margaret?"

"Oh yes, Donald. I feel better now. And Mummy
won't smack me any more?"

"No, Margaret, course not. You've asked Jesus to make you good, and if we're good Mum and Dad are happy, and then they never have to whip us, do they?"

"No," said Margaret.

"Good-night," said Donald.

"Good-night, Donald," said Margaret. "I'm so glad it's all right now."

And then silence, while Mamma crept softly downstairs, with tears in her eyes and gladness in her heart, happy to know that her darlings had already found a friend in Jesus and were learning so soon to roll their burden upon the Lord.

The Man Who Always Said His Prayers

JOHN and his mother were in a London restaurant. It was packed with people and they were waiting more or less patiently to be served. At last the waitress appeared, bringing them their dinner.

John, who was very hungry, seized his knife and fork and prepared to eat. Then he hesitated.

Mother had bowed her head to say grace. John looked at her, then at the people all around, and blushing just a little, took his first bite.

"You didn't forget anything, did you?" asked Mother, as she started to eat.

"No," said John, "but I didn't like to; everybody was looking at me."

"But what does that matter?" asked Mother. "If it is right to thank God for our food at home, surely we should do it everywhere we go."

"But the people stare so," said John. "It makes me feel so uncomfortable."

"It shouldn't," said Mother. "We should never be afraid of people when we are doing right."

John went on eating vigorously, and in silence. The matter was apparently forgotten.

But when John asked for a story that night, Mother had one ready for him. Indeed John was sur-

41

prised how quickly Mother thought of one this time, for sometimes she took a long time to do so.

"This is the story," said Mother, "of the man who always said his prayers."

"What, prayed all day long?" asked John.

"Oh no," said Mother. "But he always said his prayers no matter what people said of him or how they treated him. His name was Daniel, and it was his practice to pray three times a day, once in the morning when he got up, once at dinner-time, and once just before he went to bed."

"That's once more than we do," said John.

"Yes," said Mother, "and that is perhaps why he was such a good man.   Anyhow, that was his habit. Now, in those days people did not live in houses like ours.   There was no glass in their windows, and unless the curtains were drawn people could readily see in.   So it often happened that passers-by saw Daniel praying in his room.   They did not disturb him, but they peered in wondering, perhaps, just what he was doing.

"One day some of his enemies happened to pass the window and, seeing Daniel at prayer, thought of a new way of causing him harm.   Having much influence with the king, they went to him and said, 'We want you to make a law that if anyone asks a petition of any god or man other than yourself during the next month he shall be cast to the lions.' Of course it was a very foolish decree, but the king, feeling very flattered at the idea, signed it, and it became law.

"At once the law was published all over the kingdom, and people began to wonder just how it would work out.   Many knew about Daniel's habit of saying his prayers three times a day, and they said to each other, 'I wonder what he will do now?'

"Early next morning people began to gather round Daniel's house. 'Will he pray at his window, as usual?' was the question on everybody's lips, 'or will he obey the king's decree?'

"More and more people came. Every eye was fixed on Daniel's window.

"At last the hour of prayer arrived. Daniel knelt in his usual place and prayed as he had always done. He made no attempt to draw the curtains and hide himself, though he could easily have done so."

"Did he know about the law?" asked John.

"Oh, yes," said Mother, "he must have done. He was chief ruler of the land, next to the king, and his servants would surely have brought him word about what his enemies had persuaded the king to do in his absence. That is why what he did was so brave. He realized what he might have to suffer for saying his prayers, but he said them just the same.

"How the people must have stared as they saw him kneeling there! I expect some said, 'Brave man!' and others, 'How dare he disobey the king!'

"His enemies were there, too, and they at once ran off to tell the king. They were overjoyed that Daniel had so soon fallen into the trap they had laid for him.

" 'Do you know,' they said to the king, 'that fellow Daniel has actually dared to defy your decree already. He is saying his prayers as usual now. You must have him arrested and cast to the lions at once.'

"Now the king thought a great deal of Daniel. He knew that Daniel was a good man and he valued his

Daniel in the lions' den.

wise counsel in caring for his kingdom. The last
thing he wanted was to see Daniel cast to the lions.
He felt so sorry that his foolish pride had led him to
sign the decree. If only he had thought about it more
he would have realized that his faithful minister would
be affected by it. Now, however, he could do nothing. Try as he would he could find no way out.
Having signed the decree he had to abide by it. So
at last, very reluctantly, he gave orders that Daniel
should be cast to the lions.

"The soldiers went round to Daniel's house and
carried him off. Dense crowds of people watched him
being taken away and followed him to the den of lions.
They saw the great stone in front of it rolled back, and
the poor man thrown in. Most of them expected that
he would be consumed in a moment, but a great
surprise awaited them.

"Even in the den of lions, with the great beasts
pacing up and down around him, Daniel prayed to
God. And God heard and answered him.

"All that night the king could not sleep, and very
early in the morning he went alone to the den of lions
and cried sorrowfully, 'O Daniel, servant of the living
God, is thy God, Whom thou servest continually, able
to deliver thee from the lions?'

"Then to his great joy the king heard a familiar
voice coming from the den, and Daniel said, 'My God
hath sent His angel, and hath shut the lions' mouths,
that they have not hurt me.'

"At this the king was ever so glad and at once
commanded that Daniel should be taken out of the pit
and his enemies thrown in. After that he made
another decree, which he sent out to every part of his

kingdom, telling of the power of the great God Whom Daniel served and worshipped. 'I make a decree,' he wrote, 'that in every dominion of my kingdom men tremble and fear before the God of Daniel: for He is the living God, and steadfast for ever, and His kingdom that which shall not be destroyed, and His dominion shall be even unto the end. He delivereth and rescueth, and He worketh signs and wonders in heaven and in earth, Who hath delivered Daniel from the power of the lions.'

"And so," concluded Mother, "because Daniel was faithful in saying his prayers every day, no matter who was looking at him, or what he might have to suffer for it, this beautiful testimony of the king to the power of Daniel's God was sent out to all the people of the world. Who can tell how much good it accomplished?"

John was silent for a little while.

"I wish I had said my grace at dinner-time to-day, Mother," he said presently. "I think Daniel would have done."

"You must remember it next time," said Mother.

And he did.

When Dick Ran Away

DICK was upset again.

In fact, it seemed that he was always getting upset about something. If he did not get his own way all the time he would carry on in the most ungentlemanly manner. And if anyone corrected him he would either snarl an angry reply or else wander off into some corner and sulk.

When in these very bad moods he would mutter threats about running away from home. Although he was only ten years old he had a very big opinion of himself and was quite sure he was well able to look after himself in the world. That he owed his father and mother anything for all their loving care over him never seemed to enter his mind. He only wanted to get away from all restrictions, away to some place where he would be able to do just as he pleased.

He was thinking these thoughts just now. Daddy had asked him to cut the lawn just as he had planned to go out and play ball with the boy next door. How he hated cutting the lawn! Why should he cut the lawn? He wished there were no lawn to cut. He would give anything to get away from the sight of it. But he did cut it, his little soul meanwhile seething with rebellion.

That afternoon his wishes were crossed again. Several times, in fact. As a result he became rude and cross and finished up with a good spanking and being sent early to bed. He did not say his prayers, and instead of going to sleep, planned what seemed to him a glorious dash for liberty. He would get up when everyone else had gone to bed, creep out of the house, and run far, far away. He was not quite sure where he would go, or what he would do when he got there. He just had one all-absorbing desire to get away where there would be no lawn to cut and where he wouldn't have to give up things for his brothers and sisters, nor be expected to do what he was told.

At last, when all was still, and he felt sure that everyone must be fast asleep, he decided to put his plan into action.

So he jumped softly out of bed, put on his clothes very quietly, took his purse out of the cupboard—he was very proud of this, for it contained half-a-crown —and crept out of his room.

As he passed the bed where his baby brother was lying asleep, it occurred to him that he would never see little Tiny again, so he bent over and kissed him; and a strange lump came into his throat and he couldn't swallow very well. He kissed Tiny twice and then went out of the room. Going past the room where Daddy and Mamma were asleep, he thought he would like to say good-bye to Mamma anyway. He wasn't quite sure about Daddy because he had made him cut the lawn. But, really, he wouldn't like not to see Mamma any more. He began to wonder whether he should run away after all. Then the old, hard spirit came back and he went downstairs. Very quietly he put on his overcoat and gloves, drew the bolt of the front door, and went out into the cold night air.

He stopped on the doorstep. This was hardly what he had dreamed about. It was too dark for one thing and too cold for another. Bed began to seem very nice. Perhaps, after all, it would be better to go back.

But no, he wouldn't. He closed the door. There was a snap! and he realized that he couldn't go back now even if he wanted to. That wasn't a nice feeling at all. He wished he hadn't let the door close quite so tightly.

It was done now, however, and on he must go. He went down to the front gate and out into the street. There was nobody about. All was very quiet and still. The sky was black, and the only light came from the street lamps. It was all very eerie. Dick didn't like it a bit. If the door wasn't locked, he told himself, he would go back to bed.

He walked some distance down the street, and as the cold night air cooled his fevered mind he began to realize more and more what a foolish enterprise he had started on. "If the boys at school get to hear about this," he said to himself, "they will tease me for the rest of the term." The very thought of his school chums discovering his foolhardiness made him turn round suddenly and make for home.

He had not gone far, however, when he nearly jumped out of his skin as a heavy hand was laid on his shoulder and a strange voice spoke to him.

"What are you doing out at this time of night?" asked the policeman.

Dick was paralysed with fright. He had not ex-

VII B.S. 4

pected this.   Words would not come.   He merely struggled to get free.

"You'd better come along with me," said the policeman.   "You've been up to some mischief, it seems."

"I haven't, I haven't," gasped Dick. "I've made a mistake, that's all, please sir."

"I should think you have made a mistake, being out here at one o'clock in the morning.   You can tell me all about it when we get down to the station."

"You're not going to take me to the police station, are you?" cried Dick, more frightened still.   "Let me go home!   I want to go home."

"You'll go home, all right," said the policeman, "after we have had a little chat by the fire."

And so poor Dick found himself for the first time in his life on his way to the police station!

There he was asked more questions in ten minutes than any teacher had ever asked him at school.   Afterwards he was given a very rough mattress to lie on until the morning.   He didn't sleep at all.   He was too terribly frightened, wondering what the policeman was going to do with him and what his Daddy would say.   How he wished he had never started out on such a foolish adventure!   How comfortable his own little bed seemed!   And there was no Tiny to look at when he woke up, and no Mamma to come to him when he called.   What a night it was!

Morning dawned at last.   Very early the policeman came and told him to put his clothes on.   Together they walked back home.   How very small poor Dick felt!   What a home-coming!   What would the others say?

Daddy, unshaven and in his pyjamas, opened the door.

"What in the world——" he began.

The policeman explained and departed, smiling. Dick jumped into Daddy's arms and hugged him, pyjamas and all. They didn't say much to each other, but just walked up the stairs like that to tell Mamma all about it.

For breakfast that morning Mamma gave everybody an egg each in addition to their porridge, and opened a new pot of marmalade besides, for she said that as her little prodigal son had returned she surely must kill the fatted calf.

And as for Dick he said very earnestly that he had run away for the last time in his little life and that he certainly wouldn't talk about doing so again.

Nebuchadnezzar sees four persons in the fire.

Faithful Unto Death

As Edith came in from school Mother saw at once that something was wrong.

"What is the matter, dear?" she asked. "You look as though all the troubles in the world were on your shoulders."

"Oh dear!" cried Edith, "I'm tired of them for ever teasing me, day in, day out. It's always the same."

"What do they say to you?" asked Mother. "You musn't mind a little teasing. Every little girl gets teased at school some time or other."

"Oh, it isn't just ordinary teasing," said Edith. "It's the way they will keep calling me 'Jewy-Jew' just because I keep the Sabbath. Why can't they leave me alone?"

Mother sat down and drew Edith on to her lap.

"Let me tell you a story," she said, "then you will feel so much happier about it. It's about three boys who were taken away into a foreign country and made to live with people who didn't believe as they did. It was very hard for them. They wanted to remain loyal to God and His laws, but everyone around them was a heathen and a worshipper of idols. If they ever dared to speak of their religion the people of the land would laugh at them. Because they tried to be good the people would do all they could to annoy them and find fault.

53

"Then one day they were brought to a very severe test. The king of that country took it into his head to make a great idol. It was a very large one, all of pure gold. He was very proud of it and determined that everyone in his kingdom should bow down to it. So he issued a decree that on a certain day all the people should gather on a great plain around the idol, and at a given signal fall down on their faces before it. To make sure that everyone would obey him he threatened that, if any should fail to bow down to it, he would have them cast into a red-hot furnace.

"The three boys realized that the biggest test of their lives had come. They could not avoid it, for everybody was sent out on to the plain. Not a soul was allowed to remain behind in the city. So there they found themselves, in the midst of a vast concourse of people, facing the great golden image that stood in the centre of the crowd. How their hearts must have beaten as they waited for the signal to be given! People who knew them whispered together, wondering what they would do now.

"At last the king's band began to play. There was a great shout and the people in their tens of thousands threw themselves prostrate upon the ground. Over all that vast plain only three figures remained erect. They could not have been more conspicuous. People began to look up at them out of the corners of their eyes. The news spread rapidly from end to end of the multitude. 'The three Hebrew boys have refused to bow down to the king's image.' What excitement!

"There must have been a tremendous stir. Everybody knew what the penalty was, and they waited to

see what the king would do. Meanwhile the three
boys stood there, their faces pale and set, bravely
awaiting their fate.

"The king sent for them. He was in a furious
temper. He asked them what they meant by disobey-
ing his decree and warned them again of the fiery furnace. Respectfully, but firmly, the boys replied, 'Our
God Whom we serve is able to deliver us from the
burning fiery furnace, and He will deliver us out of
thine hand, O king. But if not, be it known unto thee,
O king, that we will not serve thy gods, nor worship
the golden image which thou hast set up.'

"At this the king was still more furious and told
his soldiers to heat the furnace seven times hotter than
usual. Then the three boys were bound and cast into
it. That must have been a terrible moment for them.
But they did not waver, not even when they felt the
fierce heat of the fire upon them.

"Then a wonderful experience came to them. The
fire burned their bonds, but left them untouched. Suddenly Jesus Himself appeared among them and walked
with them in the midst of the fire. The king saw the
four figures walking there and was terrified. He called
to the boys to come out of the furnace and trium-
phantly they strode forth and the record says, that
not 'an hair of their heads was singed, neither were
their coats changed, nor the smell of fire had passed
on them.'

"The whole concourse of people witnessed the
miracle and must have been greatly impressed. As
for the king he admitted that the God Whom the boys
served was greater than his image. 'There is no other
God that can deliver after this sort,' he said. And so,

because those boys were faithful, and were not afraid to suffer even death for what they believed, the whole nation was blessed and even the king was led to see the folly of his idolatry."

"I think I can see what you mean," said Edith, much brighter now.

"I'm sure you can," said Mother. "You are God's little witness to His truth at your school. He may have no other there, for aught you know. You must be loyal to Him at all costs. You know that the Sabbath is right, and that God in His Word commands us to keep the seventh day holy. The others may tease you about it, but that doesn't matter. It only makes plain that you are God's little witness there. And if you are loyal to Him in spite of all the unkind things they say and do, why, Jesus will walk with you at school as He did with the boys in the fiery furnace long ago."

"I think I feel better about it now," said Edith. "I'll try to be as brave as those three boys."

STORIES

for

TINY TOTS

Feeding the horse.

© Topical

Feeding the Animals

Do you like feeding animals?

It is great fun, isn't it? And the animals seem to like it just as much. How Fido does jump about when you talk about dog biscuits! How pussy will purr when you pour out her saucerful of milk!

Then, of course, there are the chickens down the garden. Don't they run when they see you coming with their food!

And there's that robin redbreast who comes and sits on the fence opposite the back door waiting for the crumbs he hopes you are going to throw out. Doesn't he look excited and pleased!

Of course, you have been down to the pond sometimes to feed the ducks or the baby swans. Everyone likes throwing pieces of bread to them. The little children in our picture have been doing that, I think. And the ducks have gobbled it all up and are quacking loudly for more.

Have you ever been allowed to feed a horse? The little girl in our picture is lucky, isn't she? I think she looks just a little bit frightened about it though, don't you? At any rate she is keeping her hands as far as she can from his mouth. But she certainly seems happy about it, and so does the horse. There is a little twinkle in his eye, I think.

If you are fortunate enough to live near a zoo you have probably enjoyed yourself many a time feeding the animals there. What a noise the lions do make just before feeding time, don't they? But I think the

Down by the pond.

© P. Phillips

sea-lions make more still. And how they do jump when the keeper comes along with his pail of fish! Splosh! they go into the water, trying to be first to get the food. Rather greedy of them, isn't it?

Of course you have fed the monkeys, haven't you? Don't they love monkey-nuts! And the bears, how they love buns! I once saw a big white polar bear at the London Zoo sit bolt upright, open his mouth in a broad smile, and actually wave his right paw at me— all to persuade me to throw him a piece more bun.

The little children in our picture are feeding the reindeer. These animals seem just as pleased as the others to receive something from their little visitors. The little boy in front is very brave, isn't he? His big brother at the back seems rather scared.

Giraffes are very particular about their food; perhaps because it has such a long way to go down. But they like children to feed them, nevertheless. So do the elephants, big as they are. Try putting a bun on the tip of Mr. Elephant's trunk and see what happens.

Feeding helps so much in making wild animals tame. A big game hunter once caught a tiger in a trap. He wanted to bring it alive to England. For the first few hours of the trip the captive animal made a terrible fuss, rushing about his cage and roaring terribly. Then as he discovered that his food came to him regularly without any trouble he began to quieten down and at last became quite docile.

Of course, it is possible to feed animals too much. Like boys and girls, they get indigestion if they over-eat. Many a good dog has been spoiled because his youthful master has tried to show his affection for him by feeding him at all hours of the day.

On the other hand, it often happens that our pets are forgotten and left to go hungry because we are too busy to think about them. Have you ever forgotten to give your dog his supper? Or come back late in the evening to remember that your chickens have gone to roost without their evening meal? Ever left the rabbit hungry because you were playing football, and didn't think about it?

Well, if you have, it's too bad. How would you like to go to bed cold and hungry, or be told on coming in from morning school that Mamma has been so busy reading a book she has neglected to get your dinner ready? You wouldn't like it a bit, I know.

We should treat our faithful animal friends as we would like to be treated ourselves. I think the Golden

A happy time at the Zoo. © Topical

Rule applies to them as well as to us, don't you? Certainly, if we follow it we shall discover new sources of happiness and gather round us a host of loyal and devoted friends who will make life ever more interesting and beautiful day by day.

Mabel sets her seeds. © Topical

Helping Daddy

DADDY was down the garden setting some seeds in the ground. They were pea seeds and Daddy was making a very straight row so that when the peas came up they would look nice.

Mabel was watching Daddy and she thought that she would like to set some pea seeds too.

So she got her little fork and dug a hole in the ground. Then she came to Daddy and said, "Please, Daddy, give me some of your pea seeds for me to set."

So Daddy gave her some of his pea seeds and Mabel dropped them into the big hole she had made and covered them over with earth. Daddy looked round to see what she was doing and he said, "Why, my little girl, those seeds are too far down. They will never be able to find their way up."

"Well," said Mabel, "I 'specks they will grow all right, but I think I will set some more in case they don't."

But Daddy had already set all the pea seeds and Mabel was very disappointed. And do you know what she did?

You could never guess. Well, when Daddy wasn't looking she went over to where he had set his row of peas and, poking her hands down into the earth, fetched up some of the seeds. Just then Daddy looked round and he said, "Oh, you naughty little girl! Whatever are you doing?"

"Just getting some more seeds," said Mabel, "'cos I didn't have enough."

"Well, I never did!" said Daddy. "Digging up my nice new row of seeds. That is naughty of you, Mabel."

"But they will grow just as well here as there," said Mabel, digging another deep hole and dropping in the seeds she had taken from Daddy's row.

"No, they won't," said Daddy. "You mustn't take seeds that do not belong to you. If you had left them where they were we should have had some lovely peas from them one day. But now they will never grow."

When the spring came Daddy and Mabel were down the garden again.

"What a lovely row of peas!" said Mabel.

"Yes," said Daddy, "it's just spoiled by a little gap up at the other end, isn't it?"

"Yes," said Mabel, "is that where I took some out?"

"Yes," said Daddy, "and where are they now?"

"I can't see them anywhere," said Mabel.

"No," said Daddy, "and you never will. Nobody ever gains by doing naughty things. I think they must have gone down the other way."

And they had.

Tom's Slippers

TIM was not in a very good frame of mind. He was inclined to "grizzle"—if you know what that means. It is sort of half-way between a cry and a grunt. Little boys get the complaint every now and then, usually when they want what they can't get or when they don't like what they do get.

The cause of the grizzling this time was a paint-box. You see, Tim had a paint-box and Tom, his brother, had a paint-box. Unfortunately, Tom had finished all the paints in his box. He liked to pour lots of water into his paints and then paint big pictures on Daddy's newspaper. So, of course, his paint-box was soon empty.

That being the case, Tom began to cast longing eyes at Tim's paint-box; and Tim, having painted smaller pictures than Tom, and so having a few paint-cups left that were not empty, thought it wasn't fair that he should share them with Tom.

Whereupon there was a strong difference of opinion about the matter. Tom made a grab at Tim's paint-box, and Tim sought to defend his possessions by jabbing Tom in the nose with his paint-brush. Altogether it was a very unseemly quarrel and matters might have got very much worse had not Mamma suddenly come on the scene and bundled both boys out into the garden to cool off.

But Tim did not forget his troubles and grizzled all the time about what Tom had done or tried to do.

67

He told Tom that he would never let him have his paints, never.

At last they were called in for tea. And then something else went wrong.

They had to change their garden shoes and put on their slippers when they came into the house, but when they started to do so poor little Tim discovered that his slippers were missing. He looked high and low, but they were nowhere to be seen.

By this time Tom had his slippers on, which only made Tim more desperate.

"Huh, huh, huh," he began to grizzle again, "I can't find my slippers. Huh, huh, huh!"

Once more he looked in every corner he could think of, wandering around disconsolately in his socks crying, "Huh, huh, huh, somebody's got my slippers."

And then a beautiful thing happened.

As poor little Tim came into the dining-room again crying, "Huh, huh, huh," Tom took off one of his slippers and said, "Here you are, Tim, we'll have one each."

Tim's face lit up with a happy smile as he eagerly seized the slipper and put it on his left foot. Then, hand in hand, they went off together to hunt for Tim's slippers. How funny it was to hear them wandering round the house, clod, thump, clod, thump, clod, thump—each with one foot in a slipper.

Suddenly there was a cry of joy. Tim's slippers had been found! In their usual place, of course, under his bed. With great rejoicing they came downstairs together, hands clasped and faces radiant.

After tea they were allowed to stay up a little while,

as Mamma wanted to finish the ironing before putting them to bed.

So they started painting Daddy's newspaper again and two brushes could be seen dipping vigorously, and with perfect peace and harmony, into Tim's paint-box.

Tom's happy little thought had driven all the grizzles away.

"Tod poked the letter into the box."

© Topical

The Letter to Mamma

MAMMA was very ill and some people had come in a strange motor-car with a red cross on it and carried her away to hospital.

Poor little Ted and Tod were very sad and lonely. They had never felt so lonely before. How they did long for Mamma to come back again! Every time a motor went by they would run to the window to see whether the motor-car with the red cross on it had come back again. Poor little Tod cried himself to sleep every night.

"Mamma said we were to write to her often," said Ted, one day. "Shall we do it now?"

Tod said "Yes," so they started. Tod found some paper and a bottle of ink. When he opened the ink-bottle the stopper ran round all over the paper and made a big black mark. So they decided to write the letter in pencil.

"Mamma won't mind the blots, I expect," said Ted. "Now what shall we say?"

"Tell her I want her to come back soon," said Tod.

"I will," said Ted. "And of course we must tell her we want her to get better."

So they wrote, and here is the letter:
"Dear, darling Mamma,

"Please come back soon. We hope you are getting better. We love you so much. We want you home again. Tod has lost a button off his coat. You

must not get sick any more. Pussy has got some kit-
tens. We say our prayers every night. We ask Jesus
to make you better. Tod says come back soon and so
do I. With lots of love and kisses from your lonely
little boys,   Ted and Tod.''

And then they stuck down the envelope, got a
stamp from Auntie, and went out to post the letter in
the pillar-box.

Tod said he wanted to post the letter but when
they got to the pillar-box they found he could not quite
reach the place where the letters go in. So Ted lifted
Tod as high as he could and Tod poked the letter into
the box.

And when Mamma opened the letter next morning
she was so pleased she said she felt better already.

Cutting the Wrong Grass

LITTLE James is one of the dearest little baby boys you ever saw. If you could see him I am sure you would want to pick him up in your arms and hug him. But, well, he is a real boy, even though he is so young, and just as full of mischief as boys usually are.

You'll never guess what he did the other day. Every time I think about it I laugh all over—though I suppose I should cry because of what nearly happened.

Well, it was this way: Master James was in his garden with his daddy. I chanced to be quite near and so saw everything.

His daddy was cutting the lawn with a mowing machine. On the lawn was a pair of shears.

Baby James, anxious to help his daddy, picked up the shears and started cutting the grass.

"Look, Daddy!" he cried, "I'm helping you cut the grass."

Daddy looked and smiled his thanks, but told him he should not play with the sharp shears.

Just then Prince ran on to the lawn.

Prince is the dog, you know, a little dog with lots of hair—the kind of dog that really would look nicer if he could go to the barber and have a bob or a shingle.

At any rate little James seemed to think so for, leaving his grass-cutting, he gave chase to Prince, shears in hand.

Unfortunately, he missed Prince's hair and caught his hind leg, and what might have happened if little James's arms had been stronger I don't like to suggest.

But the sight of that poor little dog parading across the lawn with the shears attached to his hind leg, and with the astonished little James looking on, is one that I shall not soon forget!

Of course, James's Daddy saw it, too, which was rather unfortunate for James. What happened next it wouldn't be fair to tell you, but I rather think James will try to remember in future that it is always best to do what Daddy says, and to do it at once.

Oh, by the way, I should add that Prince still has four legs.

A Chick Tragedy

Now Billy and Bunty were two very little boys, just old enough to know that when Mamma said "No" she meant "No" and that when she said "Yes" well, everything was all right.

Just now they were bothering Mamma a bit in the kitchen, trying to float bits of sticks in the wash-tub, and things like that, until at last Mamma sent them helter-skelter into the garden.

"You can play anywhere you like," said Mamma, throwing their ball out to them, "but do be good. And mind, whatever you do, don't let the baby chicks out."

"All right, Mamma," said the boys. "We'll be very good."

"May we go and look at the baby chicks?"

"Oh yes," said Mamma, "but don't open the door of their run."

"All right, Mamma," said Billy and Bunty, running on to the lawn with their ball.

For quite a long time they played very happily together on the grass. Then they began to wander very slowly down the garden towards the chickens. There were lots of things to interest them on the way. A big furry caterpillar was crawling over a cabbage leaf. A little sparrow was trying to take a bath in a puddle in the path. Billy and Bunty watched them with great interest.

By the time they reached the house where the baby

Just out!   © Rural Life Photos

chicks were kept they had quite forgotten all that Mamma had said to them.

"What dear little things!" said Billy.

"They look all fluffy like baby puss-cats," said Bunty.

"I'd like to stroke one, wouldn't you?" said Billy.

"Yes," said Bunty, "let's try to catch one."

So they opened the door and stretched in their little arms as far as they would go. Bunty caught one first.

"Now get one for me," said Billy.

Bunty passed his over to Billy and made another grab. He caught another. Then they stood together stroking their little pets and feeling very happy.

After awhile they got tired of this and popped the baby chicks back into their house. Then they strolled very leisurely up the garden again, played ball on the lawn, and at last arrived at the kitchen door about tea-time.

"So here you are again, darlings," said Mamma. "You have been good boys all the afternoon!"

"Yes, Mamma," said Billy and Bunty, "we've been very good boys."

Then they had their tea and went to bed.

In the morning, when Mamma came back from feeding the chickens she had a very sad look on her face.

"There are two baby chicks dead," she said.

"Oh dear!" said Billy and Bunty together. "What a pity!"

"Yes," said Mamma. "Someone must have left the door of their house open. They must have hopped out and then not been able to get back again. They must have just died of the cold."

"Poor baby chicks!" said the boys.

Billy looked at Bunty and Bunty looked at Billy. They seemed to remember something about it.

Mamma noticed the look.

"I suppose you didn't touch the chicken-house yesterday afternoon," she said.

Again Billy looked at Bunty and Bunty looked at Billy. They were very quiet. A big tear jumped out of the corner of Bunty's eye and Billy looked very sad.

"I think you were very naughty little boys," said Mamma.

"We're very sorry," said Billy.

"And we won't do it any more," said Bunty.

"I'm afraid I shall have to ——" began Mamma.

But before she could say just what she was going to do, two pairs of arms were thrown round her neck and two little tearful voices were pleading for forgiveness.

And then, well, what could Mamma do then?

So they went down the garden and buried the baby chicks together.

Four Pots of Jam

TUBBY and Toby had just returned home from London. They were very excited—and very tired, though they wouldn't admit it—for they had spent the whole day with Mamma, walking round a wonderful exhibition. They had seen so many interesting things that when they started to tell Daddy about them all they got quite mixed up.

Then they began to bring out the treasures they had gathered during the day. Both of them had a collection of the most delightful little samples you could wish to see—tiny pieces of cheese wrapped in silver paper, packets of biscuits and cornflakes, and best of all, four dear little pots of jam.

Oh, those pots of jam! What shrieks of delight greeted their unpacking! How pretty they looked, standing on the table with the light shining through them. One was strawberry jam, one apricot jam, one blackcurrant jelly, and the other marmalade.

Tubby and Toby took quite a long time to decide how the four pots should be divided, but at last Tubby agreed to have the strawberry and apricot, while Toby took the blackcurrant jelly and marmalade.

Fancy having two whole pots of jam each! It seemed too wonderful to be true. Tubby and Toby stood them up beside their plates at tea-time so that they could keep their eyes on them. Of course, they were not very big pots, but to the happy, excited eyes of Tubby and Toby they were more precious than the biggest jars in Mamma's store-cupboard.

All through tea-time they talked about these four treasured jam-pots—how they got them, and what they were going to do with them. They were quite sure that they were going to eat all the jam themselves, and that, if they only tasted a spoonful every day, the pots would last for weeks and weeks.

Tea was almost over when Daddy said something that rather upset things a bit.

"Poor old Dad!" he said, talking as though to himself in a very disconsolate tone of voice, "Poor old Dad! He never has a jam-pot all to himself. Nobody ever gives him anything. Poor old Dad!"

Tubby and Toby stopped talking. They both looked at Daddy in surprise, questioning in their little minds whether he really meant what he said. Then they looked at their precious jam-pots.

"Here, Daddy," said Tubby, "have my pot of strawberry jam."

"You darling boy!" said Daddy. "I don't want to take your jam. It was only fun."

"But you must have it," said Tubby, setting the pot of strawberry jam down with a bang in front of Daddy's plate. "You see, I still have the apricot left."

Daddy nearly shed a tear at this, but he didn't because he was too busy watching Toby out of the corner of his eye.

The struggle was harder for Toby. He was breathing very deeply and looking hard first at one pot and then at the other. He picked up the marmalade, put it down, then picked up the blackcurrant jelly. His solemn little face showed that a big battle was being fought inside.

"Daddy," he said at last, "I think I will let you have one of mine as well. You can have the black-currant jelly."

And with that Toby plumped the pot of blackcurrant jelly down beside Daddy's plate.

"You dear, precious boys," said Daddy. "Of course I won't eat your lovely jam; but I am pleased you gave it to me. I shall remember it for ever and ever. And now I think I shall have to see what I can find."

And then Daddy started fumbling in his left-hand trouser pocket, making a sort of jingling noise that Tubby and Toby knew so well!

A borrowed overcoat.

© Topical

New Clothes for Old

WHEN you see a flock of sheep feeding peacefully in a field you probably say, "Oh, Mamma, look at the pretty sheep!" Not for a moment do you think of all the trouble the shepherds have taken to rear those sheep through the cold winter months.

If the lambs are born early in the year, before the snow has melted, many of them die of the cold. Sometimes the mother sheep dies as well. The shepherd is very sad about this, for it means a heavy loss to him, or to his master.

Sometimes it happens that a mother sheep will die and leave a baby lamb. The shepherd does not want to lose the lamb as well, but what can he do? No other sheep will take the lamb and look after it. They are not like human beings and will only look after their own little ones.

So what do you suppose the shepherd does? Well, he looks over his flock and finds a mother sheep who has just lost her lamb. He takes the poor dead lamb, removes its skin, and places it carefully over the body of the live lamb that has lost its mother. You can see the shepherd doing this in our picture. It is just like putting on an overcoat, isn't it? Anyhow, the shepherd takes the poor little orphan lamb over to the mother sheep that has just lost her own baby. She smells the lamb all over, decides that it must surely be her own, and takes it to herself.

This gives us a beautiful illustration of what the

love of Jesus does for us. Many times you must have heard the minister say in church that Jesus "covers us with the robe of His righteousness." Perhaps Mother has talked to you about this as well, and you have wondered just what she meant.

Now you can understand it so easily, can't you? We are like the poor little orphan lamb. If we love Jesus, the slain Lamb, His goodness is wrapped, like a cloak, around us and His Father accepts us, not because we are worthy of His love, but because He sees around us the glorious goodness of His own Son. Thus we are "accepted in the Beloved" and God welcomes us as His own dear children.

That doesn't mean, of course, that we can do what we like afterwards. God truly accepts us because of

Good morning!   © Topical

what Jesus has done for us, but we must ever try by His grace to live to please Him. We must not be content just to look like Jesus outside. God wants us to be like Jesus through and through.

And that is where we differ from the poor little orphan lamb. He only wears his covering a few days until his mother gets used to him. We, however, must wear the righteousness of Jesus always, daily growing in grace and beauty of character, until at last we become altogether like Him when "we see Him as He is."

NEW GLOUCESTER LTD

A happy family.

© Topical

A True Dog Story

SOME remarkable stories have been told about dogs, some of them, indeed, so strange that one wonders if they can really be true. Here is one, however, that actually happened.

A few days ago, in company with some friends, I visited a large house in the Midlands on business. The house stood in its own grounds, with a large and beautiful courtyard in front of it. One gate in this courtyard led to the farm buildings, and another opened on to the main carriage-drive.

The lady of the house, showing us round her estate, presently took us through the gate leading to the farm buildings. Immediately, from every direction, great dogs rushed upon us. They looked something like the dogs in our picture, only much bigger, and with a little more of the bloodhound about them. I had never seen so many big dogs swarming round me before. I began to think it would be as well to get back to the other side of the gate as quickly as possible.

Then a remarkable thing happened. The lady lifted her right hand and spoke just one word to the dogs.

"Obedience!" she cried.

Instantly the dogs stopped frisking about us and followed their mistress like a flock of lambs.

The lady told us that some of these big dogs were,

in fact, only puppies six months old, but that all of them were being trained with the utmost care to obey instantly her word of command.

A little later we saw the most remarkable instance of this perfect obedience that I have ever seen.

We returned to the courtyard through the other gate that led on to the main carriage-drive. The dogs had accompanied us all round the farm and as we entered the courtyard we fully expected them to follow us. But they did not.

Believe it or not as you please, those great big dogs lined up in a row across the open gateway and would not so much as put a paw into the courtyard! And, mind you, there was no gate or obstruction of any kind to keep them back.

I looked at the dogs in sheer amazement. They stood there like so many soldiers on guard. Then one of them took a pace forward and crossed the line.

Instantly a voice behind me called out the magic word, "Obedience!"

Without a moment's hesitation the offending dog went back to his place in the line!

And then another remarkable thing happened. A little terrier, the house dog, suddenly appeared on the scene. He came bounding into the courtyard, making himself quite at home. I turned in surprise to the lady.

"Oh, it's quite all right," she replied with a smile. "He is the only dog allowed in the courtyard. The others know they must stay outside."

"Well!" I said, "if that isn't extraordinary!"

And the last thing I remember about that visit is the picture of that row of giant dogs lined up, like a regiment of soldiers, across the open gateway.

As I came away I began to think what a happy world it would be if all the children in it were just half as obedient as those dogs! What a blessing it would be if when parents said, "Obedience!" all the children would instantly do what they were told without fuss or bother.

How is it in your home? Do you always obey pleasantly, happily, without a murmur?

Not always? Well, then, I want you to read this text, found in the third verse of the first chapter of Isaiah:

"The ox knoweth his owner, and the ass his master's crib: but Israel doth not know, My people doth not consider."

This means that, in God's sight, the animals are oftentimes more thoughtful and considerate than human beings. They remember who feeds them, but children sometimes do not. The animals try to serve faithfully those who look after them, but children sometimes treat Father and Mother with much rudeness and disrespect. What must God think of us when we act like that?

We mustn't let it be said that the animals are better than we, surely! Of course not! So next time Mother says, "Obedience!" I want you to think of those wonderful dogs I have told you about and, mind, you mustn't put even a paw across the line!

Part of our beautiful playground.

© Topical

Our Wonderful World

DID you ever stop to think what a wonderful world it is in which we live?

The fact is that Someone has packed it full of marvellous things great and small.

Just think how big it is.

Do you know? Well, it is a great ball twenty-four thousand miles in circumference. That means that it must be about eight thousand miles through the centre, from one side to the other. Now just think of that. The deepest coal-mine does not go down more than two miles at the utmost. To make a hole right through, so that we could walk along a tunnel to our friends in Australia, would be an immense and, indeed, an impossible task.

Over all the surface of the earth there are mighty oceans, lofty mountains, wide lakes, dense jungles, vast forests, and great expanses of desert. The oceans, lakes, and rivers teem with fish. The forests and jungles are alive with birds and beasts of all descriptions. Everywhere on land are plants and flowers innumerable. What a wonderful playground the world is for the people who live on it! And in that playground are 1,800,000,000 human beings.

When you think of the world in this way, you say to yourself, " What a big place it is!" and you feel as small as a little ant in the garden crawling about over a pumpkin.

But, big though it seems to us, the world is only a little speck of dust in the great, wide universe.

Did you ever think you would like to pay a visit to the moon? On a fine evening it does not seem so very far away, and you have sometimes thought, perhaps, that a fast aeroplane would get you there quite soon. But it wouldn't. Even though your aeroplane travelled at 100 miles an hour it would take you a hundred days of non-stop flying to get there. And so far no machine has been invented which could carry enough petrol for such a flight.

As for a journey to the sun, even though you travelled at 100 miles an hour non-stop you would be a grey-bearded man over 110 years old before you got there.

And if you were to try a trip to the nearest of the stars you would die of old age scores of years before you began to get anywhere near it.

The stars, too, are bigger than our sun, while the sun is many times bigger than our world, and yet all are moving swiftly and silently, in mighty orbits, through the realms of space.

Have you ever looked up in the sky on a calm, cloudless night? Of course you have. The heavens seem full of stars. But you can only see three thousand all together. But look through a small telescope, and you can see three million. Look through a larger telescope, and you can see endless millions more. And all of them are suns, radiating light and heat, many of them having worlds like ours revolving round them as we revolve around our sun.

How very small, then, we really are! That ant on the pumpkin makes us seem too big and important. We are more like a speck of dust on a golfball in the midst of the Atlantic Ocean.

As we gaze on all these wonders of the universe we are compelled to ask, Who made them? Who placed the stars in the sky? Who set them moving through the mighty universe? Who makes them keep perfect time so that they never bump into one another? Who gave them the power to shine?

As we ask, we know there can be only one answer. God made them. They did not create themselves. They did not evolve. They sprang suddenly into existence at the command of the Most High God. "By the word of the Lord were the heavens made; and all the host of them by the breath of His mouth. For He spake, and it was done; He commanded, and it stood fast." Psa. 33:6, 9.

And what shall we do as we think of the greatness, the wisdom, and the power, of the One Who called these millions of stars into existence, set them all in motion, and keeps them all in place by His word?

"O come, let us worship and bow down: let us kneel before the Lord our Maker." Psa. 95:6.

But the greatest wonder of all concerning this world of ours is God's care for it. By comparison with the rest of His universe it may be very small indeed, just like that golfball in the Atlantic, but God loves it more than all the rest.

Why? Who can tell? We only know He does. He tells us that He so loved our world "that He gave His only begotten Son, that whosoever believeth in Him should not perish, but have everlasting life." John 3:16.

Just think of that. Think of the infinite God in all His majesty and glory. Think of that little speck of dust on the golfball. Why should God love it? It can only be because He is infinitely wise and good and just; because His great heart of love is so full of understanding and compassion that it reaches out and touches every little life everywhere within His vast domain.

And perhaps God loves this world best of all because it alone fell into sin and yielded to the temptations of Satan. It is said that a mother loves the bad boy of the family best; not because she loves badness, but because she feels he needs the love most to bring him back to goodness and truth. So it must be with God. He loves us all, not because of our sins, but because He wants us to come back to Him.

We must never think we are too small for God to care for us. He made the stars, truly, but He painted the lily, too. He placed the great sun in the sky to send us light and heat across millions of miles of space, but He made the fire-flies also. He set the moon on high to rule the night, but He gave to tiny fishes the power to light the darkest depths of the oceans. He reared up the mighty masses of the mountains, but He designed the wings of butterflies as well.

"O Lord, how manifold are Thy works! in wisdom hast Thou made them all: the earth is full of Thy riches." Psa. 104:24.

Who tells the scarlet runner in climbing always to turn to the right and the honeysuckle and the hop always to the left?

Who tells the birds how to travel back from distant continents across strange lands and unknown seas to their old haunts? Who tells the salmon how to find the mouth of the river, even the very pool, where they were born? Who tells the baby turtle, newly hatched and far inland, how to find its way to the sea?

How is an apple made? Who planned a core in every one? Who put the pips inside the grape and gave to every fruit the power to make a tree like the one that bore it?

It is God, and God alone. "Great and marvellous are Thy works, Lord God Almighty; just and true are Thy ways, Thou King of saints." Rev. 15:3.

And all this tells us that God does care for little things. He is not so absorbed in moving the stars through space that He has no thought for us. The dust on the golfball is precious to Him. He loves little children best of all and He wants them to love Him, too.

And if they do, what a surprise He has in store for them! He tells us that, "Eye hath not seen, nor ear heard, neither have entered into the heart of man, the things which God hath prepared for them that love Him." 1 Cor. 2:9.

And when God starts planning surprises we may well expect something beyond our brightest dreams. Think of it! The hand that made the stars is preparing our heavenly home! The fingers that fashioned the fairest flowers of earth are filling that home with riches untold.

So the wonders of the world we know to-day are as nothing compared with the wonders of the world we shall know to-morrow. And that is why we should all be glad that Jesus is coming soon. For when He Who lived and died for us in the long ago returns, He will take all who love Him to His Father's gloryland. There He will reveal His choicest treasures, and tell us all the secrets He has kept from us so long. Everybody will be supremely happy. "And God shall wipe away all tears from their eyes; and there shall be no more death, neither sorrow, nor crying, neither shall there be any more pain." Rev. 21:4. "And they shall see His face." Rev. 22:5.

We surely must plan to be there, children, and the day draws near.

Note.—The companion Volumes to this book, "Bedtime Stories" (First, Second, Third, Fourth, Fifth, Sixth, and Eighth Series), can be obtained at 1/- each, or any five numbers for 4/- from the printers and publishers:

The Stanborough Press Ltd., Watford, Herts.

10M/130/432

UNCLE ARTHUR'S
BEDTIME STORIES
(EIGHTH SERIES)

With Every Good Wish

To ....

From ....

By J. S. Eland   © Autotype Fine Art Co.

Jesus blessing the children.

Uncle Arthur's
BEDTIME STORIES

(Eighth Series)

By ARTHUR S. MAXWELL

"Except ye be converted, and become
as little children, ye shall not enter
into the kingdom of heaven." Matt.
18 :3

Registered at Stationers' Hall by
THE STANBOROUGH PRESS LTD.,
WATFORD, HERTS.

CONTENTS

PREFACE

If anyone had told us eight years ago that these little story books would spread into all the world and have a circulation of over two million copies, we would have laughed them to scorn. That there should ever be an eighth series was something we did not dare to contemplate.

But here it is. As before, we have endeavoured to keep every story true to life, with a lesson that, though well wrapped up, cannot fail to be perceived. By request we have again included some stories for Tiny Tots, but we trust these will be enjoyed even by those who consider themselves quite grown up.

And again we would express our thanks to those who have written us from the ends of the earth telling of the helpfulness of these little books. We are grateful, and send forth this new volume in the hope that this also may bring blessing and happiness to children everywhere.

THE AUTHOR.

Copyright 1931
The Stanborough Press Ltd.,
Watford, Herts.

Chums.

© Rural Life Photos

Doggie Love

We all love dogs, don't we? Nice dogs, I mean.

I expect you have been looking at those two delightful little puppies on the cover page and wishing and wishing that they would suddenly become real and jump out of the picture into your arms.

I am sure I wish they would. I would be ready to rush straight down town to the post office and buy a licence for them, wouldn't you?

Dogs can be so friendly and lovable. Of course, like most boys and girls, they get up to all sorts of mischief, but you can't help loving them just the same.

Treated properly they often become the most loyal of friends, and sometimes you find that not only will they remain faithful to their human masters but they will also keep true to their doggie chums.

Which brings me to a very sad story. So get out your handkerchiefs. You may need them.

Some years ago there lived in Liverpool a dog called "Chubby" and another known as "Old Bob." They were the best of friends, eating together, playing together, and getting into mischief together. If you saw "Old Bob" alone you could be sure that "Chubby" was not far away. They were inseparable and enjoyed each other's company like twin brothers.

And then, alas, came a day of tragedy. Poor "Chubby" took ill and died. "Old Bob" couldn't understand what had happened to him. All he knew was that there was no longer any "Chubby" for him

7

to play with. He looked for him everywhere but could not find him. He called to him in his own doggie language but there was no answer.

Then he was taken out to the Liverpool Dog Cemetery, where poor "Chubby" had been buried. There was no "Chubby" for "Old Bob" to see, but somehow he understood. Next day he visited the grave again. The day after he went there again. He could not keep away from the place. And every day for three years "Old Bob" went to that tomb to mourn for his doggie friend. For aught I know he is going there still, keeping his daily vigil by "Chubby's" resting place.

I wonder what he thinks about when he's there?

"Old Bob" at "Chubby's" grave.   © Topical

And whether he has still a little hope that one day, perhaps, he will run into "Chubby" again round the corner?

Poor "Old Bob"!

Did you ever hear of such doggie love as this?

Fast Friends.

Christmas Eve.

© Topical

Barbara's Talent

"Mother!" gasped Barbara, rushing into the dining-room and flopping down in an arm-chair, "I've got to earn some money."

"My dear!" exclaimed Mother. "Whatever is the matter with the child now!"

"Yes, I must," went on Barbara. "It's most important, and I have got to earn a lot very quickly."

Mother began to look serious.

"Whatever for?" she asked.

"Well," said Barbara very excitedly, "Mr. Walters, the new superintendent, told us in Sabbath-school this morning that if we didn't give fifty pounds for missions within the next fortnight Mr. James would have to come back from India right away."

"Why, we've only just sent him out," said Mother.

"I know; that's just the trouble," said Barbara. "Mr. Walters said that everybody thought there would be enough money to keep him there. But there isn't. Something's gone wrong, he said, and the Mission Board is very hard up. So there, if we don't raise the £50 in a fortnight, well, Mr. James comes home."

"That sounds very serious," said Mother. "But, Barbara dear, we can't raise £50 in a fortnight."

"Oh no," said Barbara, "not us by ourselves.

11

Each class has agreed to raise five pounds. Each one in the class has promised to raise ten shillings."

"Have you promised ten shillings?" gasped Mother.

"Why, of course," said Barbara. "I couldn't do anything else, could I? And that's why I've got to earn some money. How can I do it, Mother dear?"

"Well," said Mother, "it's all very well for you to promise ten shillings like that, but I haven't got it to give you, dear, even if you help me ever such a lot. You know Daddy has not been earning very much lately."

"I know," said Barbara, on the verge of tears, "but I—surely—can—earn it—somehow. Er—er—I must keep my—er—promise now I've made it."

Barbara began to cry.

"Never mind, dear," said Mother, "we'll find some way out, surely. But you have taken on a difficult task and no mistake."

"I did so want to help," said Barbara.

"I know, I'm sure you did," said Mother, putting her arm round Barbara's neck. "Let's think it over a while and see what can be done."

That evening, as the family gathered round the fire for prayers, Mother read to them the parable of the talents. As the story proceeded Barbara's face grew more and more serious. She could see the man with the ten talents trading with them and earning ten talents more to give to the King. Then she saw the man with the five talents earning another five talents. And then she saw the man with one talent

burying it in the earth and having nothing—nothing
—to give to the Lord at His return.

She became very serious.

"What's troubling you, dear?" asked Mother, as
she closed the Book.

"Oh, I feel just like the man with one talent who
didn't earn anything at all. Only there's just this
difference, that I don't have one talent anyway."

"Well, Barbara, I didn't think you would take it
so much to heart. And you have talents, many of
them."

"No I haven't. I haven't any at all. I'm just no
good and I'll never be able to earn that money."

"Oh Barbara, don't be so despondent. You certainly have one talent anyway, and perhaps God will
help you to use that to His glory."

"I'm sure I haven't," said Barbara.

"You have forgotten your voice," said Mother.
"You know how beautifully you can sing when you
want to. Perhaps, who knows, you may be able to
keep your promise by singing for Jesus."

"Me?" said Barbara. "How could I? No one
would listen to a little girl like me."

"I'm not so sure," said Mother. "You seem to
have forgotten that it is nearly Christmas time and
people will listen to children then, you know: that is,
if they sing nicely and reverently."

"Do you mean that I should go out and sing carols
at people's houses?"

"Well, not by yourself exactly. But I've got an
idea. Here's Richard with his violin and Bessie, she
can sing too. I believe that the three of you might

do wonderfully well. At any rate we could think about it.''

A new light entered Barbara's eyes. Hope stirred anew within her little heart. That ten shillings she had promised seemed nearer than it had since she had reached home.

All next day they talked over Mother's idea and in the evening the three children had a practice together with Mother at the piano. They soon found

A missionary sings of Jesus to a group of natives.

that they could get along very well with several simple hymns and this made them full of eagerness to see what they could do outside.

Two evenings later they started out. And what a happy time they did have! Barbara sang as she had never sung at home. She felt she was using her one talent for Jesus. People opened their windows to listen to the clear, musical little voice that rang out on the still evening air. Richard's violin was a wonderful help, and Bessie helped a lot as well. She knocked at the doors and told the story of how they were all trying to gather money so that their missionary should not have to be brought back from India. No one could resist her sweet little smile. At every house she received something. One lady gave threepence, another sixpence, and one happy old gentleman brought a shilling out of his trouser pocket.

When at last they all reached home they were so excited and happy that Mother scarcely knew what to do with them. After counting up their money they found they had collected three shillings and ninepence halfpenny.

"Why!" exclaimed Barbara, "we shall only have to go out three or four more times to get more than I promised."

"It's wonderful," said Mother. "I prayed that God would bless you to-night, and I am sure He has. That one talent came in useful, didn't it, Barbara?"

Barbara blushed a little.

"Anyway," she said, "I am glad I shall be able to keep my promise and have something to give Him after all."

© Topical

A fast game in the playground.

"One Good Turn—"

"Good-bye, Ronny."

"Good-bye Mother."

"Be a good boy at school to-day, don't forget."

"Rather," shouted Ronny as he dashed out of the gate and down the road.

As he disappeared and Mother went into the house again, her face clouded over a little.

"I do wish Ronny would be a better boy. He is so selfish and inconsiderate. He always wants everything for himself and it's so hard to get him to do anything for anyone but himself. I wonder what I can do to make him different!"

That afternoon, just after dinner, Ronny joined in the game of cricket in the field near the school. It was a wild, jolly game, with lots of fast bowling and hard hitting. At last it came Ronny's turn to go in.

There was nothing he loved so much as a game of cricket, and to hold a bat in his hand was the height of happiness. Proudly he walked across to the wicket. Carefully he watched the first ball and with one mighty hit sent it right over to the wall of the playground. He was jubilant.

The next ball came down. Flushed with his first success he rushed out again, fully intending this time to send the ball clean over the wall into the street, and so make a name for himself the boys would never forget.

But something went wrong. Ronny could never tell

just what it was. He thought the ball hit a bump on the pitch. The others said he didn't hit it straight and that it must have glanced off his bat. What Ronny did know was that he suddenly felt a sharp pain in his forehead.

As he put up his hand he felt something wet and sticky. Poor Ronny turned very pale, and dropped the bat.

"I'm afraid I'll have to go in," he said, making towards the school.

The boys crowded round him and helped him to a chair in one of the classrooms.

"I'll be all right," he said to the others; "you carry on with the game." With that they left him.

But Ronny did not feel all right. He felt very sick. He wished with all his heart that he were at home and that Mother would come and bathe his forehead.

Just then one of the senior boys looked into the room.

"Hallo, what's the matter?" he asked in a kindly voice. "Hurt yourself?"

"A little," said Ronny, trying to look brave. "Cricket ball caught me on the forehead."

"That's too bad. Better come along with me. I'll bathe it for you, if you'll let me."

"Thanks awfully," said Ronny. "It is getting rather a mess, isn't it?"

"Oh, we'll soon have that all right," said the senior boy. "This isn't so bad as having your head knocked right off, is it?"

"No," said Ronny, smiling despite the pain.

They went into the cloakroom and there, with

a tenderness only equalled by Mother herself, the senior boy bathed the wound and bound it up with liniment from the school first-aid outfit. Then with a jolly laugh and a cheerio! he bade Ronny good-bye and rushed off to his next class.

When Ronny reached home that night he had a great story to tell.

"But wasn't he nice?" he exclaimed. "You know, Mum, I'd never spoken to him before. I can't understand why he should have been so kind to a stranger. And he is one of the big boys, you know."

"It was good of him indeed," said Mother. "I do appreciate it ever so much. You will tell him, won't you? It was a kind thing to do. I could kiss him for it! I hope you will always be as thoughtful, Ronny."

"Oh, I couldn't be as good as that," sighed Ronny.

Two days passed. Again it was evening. Ronny was due home at half-past four. But he did not come. Five o'clock passed and still no Ronny. Mother began to get angry. Then she grew anxious.

At half-past five, when Mother was just about to telephone to the police-station, Ronny turned up.

Mother was waiting for him on the doorstep.

"Ronny," she said severely, "what do you mean by coming home at this hour? Don't you know how late it is? I really can't allow——"

"It's all right, Mum, I—I—I had to walk home."

"Walk home!" said Mother in astonishment. "Walk home, indeed! Didn't you have your penny for your bus fare? I know I gave it to you this morning before you left."

"I know, Mum," said Ronny, with a twinkle coming in his eye. "You gave me the penny all right, but I gave it away."

"Gave it away!" cried Mother, more astonished still. "Whatever for?"

"I just couldn't help it," said Ronny. "You see I—er—I met one of the little boys—you know, out of the baby's class, we call it—just as I was going to get on the bus. He looked very pale and sick so I asked him what was the matter. He said he didn't feel well enough to walk home and he had lost his penny. So, well, there was nothing else to do. I—er—well—I just gave him mine and walked instead. And here I am."

"Oh, you darling boy!" cried Mother, throwing her arms round Ronny's neck and dropping some tears down the back of his new blazer.

"Why, what's the matter, Mum? It's nothing like what that boy did for me the other day. It's nothing at all."

"Oh Ronny," said Mamma, smiling through her tears, "it's just everything to me."

Geoffrey's Bandsmen

It happened on the way back from the band.
That is, the quarrel happened then.

As a special treat Geoffrey and his sister Anne
had been taken to the band one evening.

They loved going to the band and would promise
their Daddy that they would be good as angels for
weeks if only he would take them there.

Of course, as soon as the band was over they
usually forgot all about their promises.

Well, the band was over one night and Daddy,
Geoffrey, and Anne had started to walk home. Unfortunately both children wanted to hold Daddy's right
hand. A very silly thing, of course, for surely
Daddy's left hand was just as comfortable to hold as
his right hand. But there, most quarrels start over
very silly little things.

"I was there first," said Geoffrey.

"No you weren't, I was," said Anne.

"I was, you get away," said Geoffrey.

"I was, you get away," retorted Anne.

"What does it matter?" asked Daddy.

"I had your right hand first," said Geoffrey.

"No, I did," said Anne. "Anyway, it's my turn."

"No, it isn't."

"It is."

"It isn't."

"Stop it, children, do!" cried Daddy in desperation. "What will the people think of you both, making all this fuss at this time of night?"

"It's my place," said Geoffrey, taking no notice, and trying still harder to push Anne away.

"It isn't yours, it's mine," cried Anne, holding on to Daddy's hand still more tightly.

"Will you stop it, Geoffrey?" said Daddy firmly. "Come round and take my other hand at once."

"Don't want to," said Geoffrey sulkily, suddenly dropping behind. "I'll walk by myself then."

"All right," said Daddy. "And we shall not forget this next band night."

So the procession moved towards home, with Geoffrey dropping farther and farther behind and shuffling his feet along in a manner that must have made the angels weep.

It was long past bed-time when they were all indoors and Mamma hurried the children up to bed without making too many inquiries as to what had happened.

Geoffrey was soon between the sheets and it was not long before he dropped off into a troubled slumber.

Hallo! What was this? He was at the band again. Surely it could not be! But he was. And, to his utter amazement, he was the conductor. Behind him were hundreds of people, many of whom he recognized. Lots of boys from his school were there too. He felt very proud of himself. Fancy being the conductor of the band in front of all his school friends. My! Wouldn't they all like to be in his shoes? He made up his mind that he would make their very ears tingle with the wonderful music he would bring from the band that night.

Then he looked round at his bandsmen. Yes, they were all there. Were they ready to play? Yes. He tapped his baton smartly on the music holder and swelled up with pride. But nobody moved.

He tapped again. No one seemed to take the slightest notice.

"Start!" he shouted. "Can't you hear me. Start!"

At this the drummer banged his drum and the man with the trombone blew one great long note. The people behind laughed. He could hear his school friends tittering.

"Play!" he cried again. "Start! All of you start!"

He tapped furiously on the music holder.

The man with the trumpet blew a piercing blast and stopped. Then the cornets began, but they all seemed to be playing different tunes. Geoffrey was in despair. He waved his arms in an endeavour to beat time, but there was no time. Rather there were all sorts of time. The clarionets had begun now, all on different notes. Geoffrey shouted to them to look at their music, but they took no notice. Now all the rest of the players began and the confusion became terrible. It seemed as though each one was playing a tune of his own. No one took any notice of anybody but himself. Geoffrey could hear "Three Blind Mice" and "Home Sweet Home" and "Old Man River" and "Rule Britannia" all mixed up together. Every man was playing just what he liked and how he liked and any time he liked.

As for Geoffrey, the players took no notice of him

whatever. He might not have been there. And yet he felt that he was responsible. The people behind him were expecting great things of him. And this was all he could do! It was terrible, and as the din increased, Geoffrey became frantic.

"Stop!" he shrieked at them all. "Stop! Stop it I say! Can't you hear me? Do what you're told, will you! Stop! Stop! Stop!"

"There, there," said Mamma, putting her hand on his forehead. "It's all right, dear, don't worry any more."

Geoffrey sat bolt upright in bed.

"So I'm not at the band after all," he said.

"At the band?" laughed Daddy. "You're in bed."

"Oh!" said Geoffrey. "You should have heard them. They just wouldn't do what I told them, Daddy. They were so obstinate. They just played their own tunes as loud as they could and wouldn't take a bit of notice when I shouted at them."

"Who?" asked Daddy.

"The bandsmen, of course. Didn't you hear the noise?"

"Well, no, I can't say I did," said Daddy. "I heard a noise, and I also heard someone acting like that on the way back from the band last night."

"Oh—er—yes," said Geoffrey, waking up fully at last. "I wonder if that's why I dreamed that dreadful dream."

"I should think it was," said Daddy.

"Well, I never did," said Geoffrey, as he dropped back on his pillow and went to sleep.

Geoffrey's dream was not forgotten in the morning and Daddy found it very useful later on when the old trouble began to come back again.

For when Geoffrey ever showed any signs of grumpiness or disobedience after that, all Daddy had to say was, "How about your bandsmen, Geoffrey?"

It always had a wonderful effect!

Shackleton's famous ship, the "Quest." © Topical

Why Mary Cheered Up

"There," said Mary, flinging her school satchel down on the kitchen table, "I'm never going to try again."

"Why, Mary dear, whatever has happened?" asked Mother. "You were so happy when you went off to school this morning."

"Maybe I was," said Mary disconsolately, "but I'm not now."

"But why, dear?"

"Teacher put up the examination results to-day and I'm twelfth again. I did so want to be top this time."

Mary buried her face in her hands and began to cry.

"Cheer up," said Mother coming over to Mary's side and putting one arm round her neck. "It might have been much worse, you know. Why, you might have been bottom, and that would have been terrible, wouldn't it?"

"I suppose it would," said Mary, "but I'm never anything else but twelfth. I simply can't get top. I've never had a prize and I suppose I never shall. I'm just a dull, stupid dunce, that's what I am, and I shall never be any good at all."

"Why Mary, dear, you'll be lots of good some day. And there are some subjects in which you have had nearly full marks. Didn't you get ninety-five per cent in botany the other day? That should cheer you up."

"It doesn't. Nothing cheers me up," wailed Mary.

"Let me tell you a story then," said Mother. "You've heard of Mr. Baldwin, once Prime Minister of England?"

"Yes," muttered Mary.

"Well, do you know, when he was a boy and took the entrance examination at Harrow he failed!"

"Did he!" said Mary.

"He surely did," said Mother. "And another boy who failed in that same examination was called Freddie Smith. When he grew up he became Lord Birkenhead, one of the greatest lawyers of his time."

"Perhaps there's hope for me yet," said Mary, brightening up a little.

"Let me tell you some more," continued Mother. "You've heard of Lord Clive, haven't you? You know, the founder of the British Empire in India."

"Yes."

"Well, it is said of him that he was the despair of his teachers when at school. As for Lord Nelson, when he went to school at Norwich, he was a very poor scholar. I don't suppose his teacher ever thought he would win Trafalgar or the battle of the Nile."

"I don't suppose he did," said Mary.

"Then there is Sir Ernest Shackleton," went on Mother, "that noble explorer who went to the South Pole. You would hardly believe it, Mary, but as a boy he never rose high in his school and couldn't apply himself to his books at all."

"Fancy all those great men being like me," said

Mary, with a smile beginning to curl round the corners of her mouth.

"There are lots more people like you, dear. You may not have heard of Viscount Byng, but he is a well-known man who for some years was London's Chief Commissioner of Police. He once told the story of how at Eton he was always bottom of his class and remained there a long time. And the boy who was bottom after him became Lord Rawlinson."

"Well, I never did!" exclaimed Mary. "I thought that all these great people must always have been top at school."

"It's a strange thing," said Mamma, "but few of them were. Many of the most useful men who have ever lived simply couldn't get on well at school. Being top at school doesn't mean that you are going to be top in everything all your life."

"But the top girls seem so bright," said Mary; "they always get good marks and can always answer so much more quickly than I can."

"Yes," said Mother, "but remember the tortoise and the hare. It isn't always the fastest that gets there first."

"I'm sure I'm as slow as a tortoise anyway," said Mary.

"Then cheer up and keep on pegging away," said Mother. "You're bound to win some day if you do."

"Oh well," said Mary, springing to her feet with new hope in her heart. "I suppose I'll have to try a bit harder next term."

And she did.

Mr. and Mrs. Sparrow looking for a home.   © Topical

A Tale of Two Sparrows

Mr. and Mrs. Sparrow were just married and they were looking for a nice place where they could build their nest.

They flew about for a long time without any success. Mrs. Sparrow was rather hard to please. Whenever Mr. Sparrow found a nice little corner that he thought would do splendidly, and came swooping down through the air to tell her so, Mrs. Sparrow would say, "Oh, that's not at all suitable for me, Mr. Sparrow. I must have something much better than that for my home."

At last Mr. Sparrow got so discouraged that he said that he wouldn't look any more and that Mrs. Sparrow, if she were so particular, had better look for herself.

Mrs. Sparrow took him at his word and said that if she couldn't find a nice place in half the time that Mr. Sparrow had taken she would know the reason why.

So off flew Mrs. Sparrow to see what she could do In a little while she returned.

"I've found such a wonderful place," she said. "It's warm and cosy, well protected from the weather, and the way in is so small that no one else will ever be able to find it and we shall be quite by ourselves with no neighbours to annoy us. You'll be able to sleep late in the morning, for there will be no other birds around to start singing too early."

31

"My dear!" cried Mr. Sparrow, "where can it be? Do show me at once. I'm so glad you have been so successful."

"Ah," said Mrs. Sparrow, "it takes me to find a home. I'll show you. You come along with me."

With that Mrs. Sparrow hopped off her perch and flew high in the air, with Mr. Sparrow following meekly at a respectful distance behind.

On and on they flew.

"Wherever are you taking me?" asked Mr. Sparrow, getting alarmed.

"You'll find out in a minute," said Mrs. Sparrow.

They were approaching a lofty church tower and Mrs. Sparrow seemed to be flying to the very top of it.

"My dear, do be careful," called Mr. Sparrow. "This is very dangerous."

Mrs. Sparrow flew on as though she did not hear him. At last she alighted where a small window had been broken at the top of the tower. In a moment she had popped inside.

Poor Mr. Sparrow followed, very alarmed and wondering what terrible thing would happen to them.

"Look," said Mrs. Sparrow. "Isn't this ideal? The very thing we have been looking for. Dry, fairly clean, and very private. I told you, Mr. Sparrow, that I would find the right place."

"But, my dear," said poor Mr. Sparrow, very agitated. "Do you think it's all right? Is it quite safe?"

"Safe!" cried Mrs. Sparrow. "Of course it's safe. Now please get busy and fetch all the straw you can find. We might as well make ourselves comfortable as soon as we can."

Very meekly Mr. Sparrow obeyed. In a little while he was back again, bringing a few pieces of straw in his beak. By this time Mrs. Sparrow had selected an attractive spot for the nest in between a number of wooden pipes. Mr. Sparrow put down his pieces of straw and went out in search of more.

It did not take them very long to build their nest and in a day or two they were quite settled down ready to enjoy a well-earned rest.

All at once something terrible happened. It was on a Wednesday evening about seven o'clock. Mr. and Mrs. Sparrow were just nice and comfortable in bed when suddenly they were awakened by a terrific noise. Groans and roars came from the big pipes, whines and shrieks from the little pipes. The whole place rocked and shook.

"My dear! My dear!" cried Mr. Sparrow. "Whatever's the matter? What can have happened? Are you quite safe?"

But Mrs. Sparrow was not there to hear. Already she was at the broken window, shrieking at Mr. Sparrow to escape for his life. And without another thought they both jumped from the top of the tower out into the dark, cold night.

Probably those poor little sparrows will never know what really happened that terrible evening. As long as they live they will tell their friends how they lost their beautiful home, recounting in awed whispers the terrors they suffered in the haunted tower.

The fact was, of course, that they had merely tried to make their nest in the church organ loft. And the awful sounds they had heard that Wednesday even-

VIII BS 3

ing were really the hymns the organist was playing for the prayer meeting.

To the people in the church the music was beautiful. "How lovely!" they all had said. "What delightful harmonies! What a wonderful organist!"

But to the poor little sparrows in the loft it had seemed like an earthquake and a hurricane combined.

All of which goes to tell us that things are not always what they seem. And sometimes children, like the sparrows, are frightened merely because they do not understand. And sometimes, too, they grumble and growl because they are not yet old enough to appreciate the meaning of things beyond them.

Perhaps you have heard a little boy say some time, "I don't like going to church. I never can understand a word the preacher says, and some of the hymns have no tune to them at all." Some day, however, he will understand the preacher and rejoice in his inspiring words. And some day the hymns that have seemed to have the least "tune" in them will be loved and prized most of all.

Perhaps, too, you have heard a little girl say, "I don't know why I have so much to put up with. I don't have the nice things other children have, and I'm always getting sick."

That is hard to understand, I admit. But when you feel like that just think that Someone is playing on the organ of your life. To you the notes sound all horrid and harsh and discordant; but the Organist knows what He is playing and some day you will understand how lovely was the tune that He composed.

So when things go wrong and you are tempted to judge quickly and unkindly, just wait a little while and think of the sparrows in the tower.

Donald—while Daddy was calling him.   © Phillips

How Donald Missed His Dinner

"Donald!"

No answer.

"Where is the boy?" said Daddy.

"It is aggravating," said Mamma, "dinner will be all spoiled."

"Well, we shall go without him if he doesn't come soon," said Daddy.

Donald was always forgetting something. In the morning he would forget where he had left his shoes the night before. Then he would forget where he had laid his cap. Then he would leave books at home which he should take to school and leave books at school which he should bring home. But his chief trouble was in keeping time. Although he had been given a fine new watch on his last birthday, still he forgot to look at it when it was most necessary that he should.

Just now he was wandering far away along the shore intent only on his shrimping net. Nothing else interested him at all. He had been told to return without fail by a quarter to one so that they could all go back in the car for dinner at their lodgings. But Donald was so happy and contented that he completely forgot his promise to return. He was entirely out of sight of the rest of the party and no one knew where he had gone. Father, Mother, sisters, brothers,

37

all called their loudest, but in vain. No Donald could be seen or heard anywhere.

"Where can he be?" asked Mamma, somewhat alarmed. "Do you think he can have hurt himself?"

"No I don't," said Daddy. "It's just a little more of his old trouble. He has got interested in something and forgotten his promise. I'm going home."

"What, and leave him behind?" asked Mamma.

"Poor Donald," said Sister.

"Serve him right," said Brother.

"I want my dinner," said Little Brother.

"Jump in the car," said Daddy.

"Oh," said Mamma, "I don't like to go and leave him behind."

"I don't," said Daddy, "but he must learn sometime that he must do what he is told and keep his promises."

"Won't you have another look for him?" pleaded Sister.

"All right," said Daddy, "I'll look once more."

Leaving the others in the car, Daddy searched again and called for Donald at the top of his voice. But no Donald appeared. When Daddy returned to the car there was a very determined look on his face. Not a word more would he say on the subject. He stepped on the accelerator and made for home and dinner.

It was a very nice dinner, but somehow no one seemed to enjoy it very much. Every now and then someone said, "I wish Donald were here," or "Wouldn't Donald like this?" and Little Brother kept repeating, "We must save some for Donald, mustn't we?"

It was two hours later before they all got back to the beach again. As the car drew up in the parking place Little Brother shrieked, "I see him, I see him."

Donald was there all right. He had come back in his own good time and found everybody gone. Never in all his life had he felt so desolate and lonesome. And they had all gone to dinner! Dinner! The very thought of it had made him ravenously hungry. He had pictured all the good things the others were eating and had become hungrier and hungrier.

It was too bad of them to go, he had thought. Then he had looked at his watch. Twenty minutes to two. "Well," he had said to himself, "I suppose I couldn't expect them to wait all this time." Then, reflecting that they would all probably return after

The tunnel with a gate.
(See story on page 51.)   © Topical

A jolly time by the sea.

© Topical

dinner he had gone and laid himself down beside a boat and tried to forget his troubles.

Donald was still gazing up into the sky when he was roused by the joyous rush of feet towards him.

"So here you are, after all," said Sister. "I am so glad you are all right."

"We had a jolly fine dinner," said Brother. "You missed something, I can tell you, by being late."

Donald tried to look as though that didn't matter at all and that he had never felt the slightest pang of hunger.

Daddy now turned up on the scene.

"We were sorry to leave you, Don," he said, "but you'll have to learn some day that keeping promises on time is a most important matter."

"It seems so," said Donald.

"It is most important," repeated Daddy.

Just then Little Brother crept close to Donald and whispered in his ear.

"I've brought you some of my dinner," he said. "It's done up in my handkerchief in my trouser pocket."

"You dear!" exclaimed Donald. "I shan't forget that anyway."

And the fact is he didn't forget the lesson either.

The Tale of a Tangle

It was holiday time and George wanted a kite.

It was not the only thing George wanted, by any means, but just for the moment it was the thing he wanted most.

"Dad," he said, "do come and look at the lovely kite they've got in the corner shop. It's just the very one I want."

"I believe it," said Dad, very disinterestedly.

"Do come and just look at it," begged George.

"I've seen lots of kites," said Dad.

"But this is a new kind," persisted George, "and I really must have it. And if we don't go soon it may be gone."

"Oh, don't be so impatient," said Dad. "There's no great hurry."

"But there is really. You see, someone will buy it if we don't. I saw a boy looking in the shop just now and I'm sure he wanted it."

"Let him have it," said Dad.

"Oh no, I couldn't," said George, getting desperate. "I simply must have that one. And after all, Dad, it's only ninepence."

Dad pricked up his ears.

"Only ninepence? And who is going to pay for it?"

"Oh I am, of course. That is—er—if you will lend me the ninepence."

42

"Rather," said Dad, "I seem to have heard that before."

George returned to the attack. He affirmed that he had never had a kite in his life; that other boys always had kites. Some had two or three. If he had a kite he would be supremely and eternally happy. He would never worry anyone ever again. Dad would be free to read his paper without any further interruption. No, Dad would not be asked to fly the kite nor wind in the string, unless he really wanted to do it. The kite would indeed become the greatest boon to the whole family that had ever been purchased. And all for ninepence, to be paid back, under solemn promise, during the next twelve months.

Either from rising interest or utter desperation Dad at last submitted to the inevitable and found himself being escorted to the corner shop.

"That's it, that's the one," cried George. "It's still there. What a blessing no one bought it while you were making up your mind, Dad."

"What a pity, you mean! By the way, it's rather small and very flimsy."

"Yes," admitted George. "A large one would really be better, but it would cost more money, you know."

"Yes, I see."

They discussed kites for twenty minutes with the lady in the shop and at the conclusion Dad found himself the poorer by two shillings.

They had decided to take a larger one and the ninepenny one was put back into the window.

George was frantic with delight.

"I'll pay you back the two shillings," he said reassuringly.

"Yes, of course," said Dad, having a vision of the debt being spread over two years instead of one.

They were just leaving the shop when Dad noticed something.

"Where is your string?"

"String?" repeated George, in dismay.

"Yes, string," said Dad with emphasis. "Got any?"

"Why—er—no," said George ruefully, "I can't say I have. I really never thought about it. Don't they give us the string with the kite?"

"Not usually. The string will cost you another sixpence."

George's face fell. "I'm afraid I shall have to borrow that as well."

Dad laughed. "I'll give you that, Son. But mind, whatever you do, don't undo that ball of string until you are ready to use it. Then wind it on a thick, round piece of wood."

"Oh, I know what to do," said George, "I can do it all right."

They left the shop and returned home. Dad had left half a crown there instead of ninepence. But he had gained something he did not expect.

At dinner time there was no sign of George.

"George!" cried Dad. "Where are you?"

Mother came in.

"It's all right," she said, "George has had just a little accident and he'll be along soon."

But George did not come along soon. Dad went to find out what was the matter. He found him in the other room with the ball of string on the floor. To be more correct, it was a pile of string. Indeed it was one appalling, heart-breaking tangle. Poor George sat on the floor beside it, picking, pulling, twisting, winding, his face meanwhile the very picture of gloom.

"Whatever does this mean?" asked Dad. "Is that the lovely ball of string we bought this morning?"

George turned his tear-filled eyes upwards, but only for an instant. Without saying a word he returned doggedly to his seemingly unending task.

"George! How did this happen? Did you undo the ball before you were ready to wind it on the stick?"

George nodded and the nod threw a tear out on the floor.

"Well," said Dad. "That was deliberate disobedience. You are a most impatient boy and you deserve to be punished."

"I am," said George.

As for the tangle, well, Mother had a go at it, Auntie had a go at it, Sister had a go at it, and, of course, Dad had a go at it; and it was not until two days later that Dad's two shillings soared into the air at the end of that ball of string.

And now every time George sees a kite in the sky he remembers his mistakes and determines to be a better boy.

A bottleful of curiosities.

© Topical

Curiosities

Hunting for curiosities is a great game. It will keep you amused for hours. That is, of course, if you find some now and then.

Perhaps you will say, What is a curiosity? Well, it is something different from the ordinary, like a stone with a hole in it on the beach. There are millions of pebbles on the beach but only a few of them have holes. That's why we like to find them, isn't it?

Of course, if you live near the seaside you can find all sorts of curiosities if you start to search for them. Strange shells, star fish, anemones, and funny little bits of seaweed.

If you live in the country there are curiosities without number in the fields and woods and hedgerows. Quaint little birds, peculiar flowers, hollow trees, and the like.

And if you are not so fortunate as to live in the country or by the sea you can get lots of fun looking for strange things on the streets or in the parks. There are hundreds of curious-looking people about, you know, and all manner of strange dresses. Then there are queer dogs and cats—dogs with long bodies and short legs, cats of strange colours, new types of motor-cars, unusual advertisements, and—all sorts of things.

If you want to have quite an exciting competition sometime, get your friend to go for a walk with you in search of curiosities. Take a notebook each and make a list of all the curious things you see, everything

Cutting an elephant's toe-nails!

© Topical

that you feel is out of the o r d i n a r y. Of course, don't put your little friend's name at the head of your list. And don't c o m p a r e your lists till you get back home. Then the one who has the longest list of real curiosities will have won the game.

The only difficulty you may find may be in deciding whether what you have put down is a "really-truly" curiosity. If you both don't agree, at least be sure you don't quarrel about it. The best way is to let your friend have the benefit of the doubt, even though you do lose the game yourself.

As you grow up, if you always keep your eyes open you will see

© Topical

The tree that grows on a roof.

all sorts of curious things and life will be so much more interesting than if you went along all the time with your eyes shut.

Just look at that elephant in the picture. There is a curiosity for you! Have you ever seen an elephant

VIII BS 4

The boy among the chimney-pots. © Topical

having his toenails cut? I don't suppose you did. To be quite exact this elephant's toenails are really being filed down, not cut. I reckon he looks far happier about it than you do on bath night when Mother gets busy with the scissors!

Now look at that great fir tree growing out of a roof! Isn't that one of the strangest things you ever saw? It's a real photograph and if ever you pass through the village of Kilmersdon in Somersetshire, you will see the tree itself—that is, if it hasn't blown down by then. By the way, the roots of this tree do not reach the ground and it draws all its life and food out of the roof itself.

Then here is another funny thing. If you live in the city of Dundee in Scotland you may often have seen this strange young man up among the chimney-pots in Preddie Street. What is he doing there, you say? He has an interesting story. For many years he rode proudly at the bows of a sailing ship. He may have travelled all over the world. Then when the ship was broken up at last, a ship's carpenter hoisted him up to the chimney-pots of his house where, instead of being washed by the waves of the sea he has been blackened by the grime and soot of the great city through half a century.

Ever seen a tunnel with a gate to it? That's a strange thing, isn't it? Fancy a train having to stop while the driver gets out to open the gate! But that doesn't really happen in this case. This tunnel, which is on the Leicester-Desford branch line of the London Midland and Scottish Railway, was actually built by George Stephenson in 1832. It is so narrow that carriage windows had to have bars placed across them to prevent passengers from hitting the tunnel with their heads should they lean out. The tunnel was closed some time ago and trains will never rumble through it again. (See picture on page 39.)

Well, this gives you a good start for your new game, doesn't it? Now keep your eyes open and see how many curiosities you can find yourself.

Where Mr. Ramsay MacDonald was born.

© Topical

Stanley's Future

"Come and sit on my knee, Stanley," said Daddy.

Stanley jumped up from his seat and ran across the room. He loved to sit on his daddy's knee still, even though he was getting to be quite a big boy.

"Well, Stanley," said Daddy, "what are you going to be when you grow up?"

"Me?" said Stanley. "I don't just know. I used to think I would like to be an engine driver, but now I think that would be too cold in winter."

"Well, what else?" asked Daddy, with a twinkle in his eye.

"Well, if I had my way," said Stanley deliberately, as though thinking it over very carefully, "I think I should like to have lots of money and do nothing at all."

"Ha, ha, ha!" laughed Daddy. "That would be nice, but where would you get the money?"

"I hadn't thought of that," said Stanley. "I suppose I should get it from somewhere and then I should buy a very fast car and a motor-boat and have a toy steam engine in my back garden big enough to carry us all."

"Oh Son, you make me laugh," said Daddy. "Cars and motor-boats do not come so easily as that. Do you know the only way most people get those nice things?"

"No, I'd like to," said Stanley.

"Then I'll tell you," said Daddy. "By hard work."

53

"Oh," said Stanley. "Isn't there a better way than that?"

"It's the best way there is," said Daddy. "There's an old saying, Stanley, 'Easy come, easy go.' It means that those who get money without working for it soon lose it. The things we appreciate most are those we work the hardest for. You know how you like to get sixpence for cutting the lawn, don't you?"

"Rather!" said Stanley. "By the way, did you pay me for cutting it last time?"

"Indeed I did," replied Daddy. "And I was going to tell you a story or two about some men who have worked hard for the good things they have. You remember Sir Thomas Lipton who died a little while ago?"

"You mean the man who built the yacht Shamrock?"

"Yes. He is known, too, for the big shops he built in many places. You would hardly believe it, but he started work as an errand boy at two and six a week! Once when he asked for a rise he was told by his employer that half a crown was all he was worth, and probably more than he was worth. But young Thomas would not let himself become discouraged. He made up his mind that he would work harder still. And it was because he worked so hard all his life that he was able to afford the money to build Shamrock."

"Tell me some more," said Stanley, getting interested.

"Well, there's the story of Lord Inchcape. In 1874 he was a penniless young clerk in an office."

"How much did he get?"

"I don't know," said Daddy. "It was only a few shillings a week. But that poor boy worked himself up and up until he is now the head of one of the largest shipping companies in the world. Probably he has a nice motor-car now, but I reckon he put in many years of hard, wearying work with long hours and little pay before he got it.

"Then there is Lord Reading, who has been Lord Chief Justice of England and Viceroy of India. Did you know that he was once a ship's boy at sea? He must have worked hard indeed to win the highest prizes that men have to offer.

"Mr. H. G. Wells, who has written a lot of books, was once an assistant behind the counter in a small draper's shop. And Mr. Bernard Shaw, who now has a world-wide reputation, used to be a telephone operator!"

"How do you know all this about these people, Daddy?" asked Stanley. "Are they friends of yours?"

"Well, I don't know them personally," said Daddy honestly, "but I've read about them, you know."

"Tell us some more then," said Stanley.

"You have heard of Mr. Ramsay MacDonald, of course. Well, he was born in a little Scottish fishing village. When he was only twelve he was sent to work on a farm. At nineteen he went to London where he earned his living by addressing envelopes by hand. He has had a hard life indeed, but now he is honoured and respected by millions in every land.

"By the way, could you recognize a Morris car if you passed one on the street?"

"Rather," said Stanley, who prided himself on his knowledge in this direction.

"Well, do you know that the man who makes those cars was knighted by the king not so very long ago largely because he had given so much money away to charities. And yet years ago he was an unknown young man making bicycles and mending broken-down cars in a suburb of Oxford.

"One day perhaps you will hear of the great scientist Sir Oliver Lodge. Very few people know, however, that he once worked as a poor lad in the Potteries and attended night classes after his hard day's work was over!

"Another man you should know about is Henry Folland. He was a Welshman, and while still a boy had the misfortune to lose an arm. It must have been an awful discouragement to him. Probably he told himself often that he would never be any good at all. But he was full of courage. He found a small job and did it well. With his one arm he worked harder than other boys with two. Gradually he worked his way up until at last, when he was still under thirty years of age, he became manager of the Raven Tin-plate Works, one of the largest tinplate works in the world. When he died it is said that he left a fortune of over a million pounds."

"And all with one arm!" exclaimed Stanley.

"Yes," said Daddy. "And you have two arms, thank God. What may you not be able to do with them!"

"It looks as though I shall have to work hard too, after all," said Stanley.

"Indeed," said Daddy. "And remember that

these great men did not merely work for money. They loved their work and became deeply interested in it. They put their work first and the money came afterwards. It is the secret of success in life, Stanley."

"Well," said Stanley with a smile, "I'll have to think it over. I'm not sure now whether I shall be a Prime Minister or a lawyer or a Viceroy or a shopkeeper."

"Anyway," said Daddy, "you still have a little time to decide."

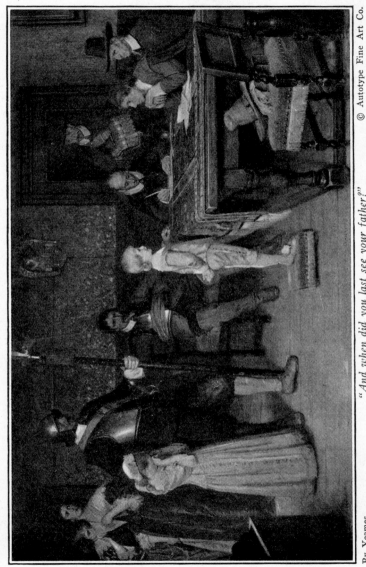

By Yeames

"And when did you last see your father?"

© Autotype Fine Art Co.

Brave Boys

Not long ago two young boys were playing on the bank of a river in the north of England. All of a sudden the smaller one fell in and was swept away by the tide. Instantly, without a moment's thought for himself, the other boy jumped in to save his brother. Neither could swim, and both were drowned.

Terribly sad, wasn't it? But what a noble boy was that older brother!

Every day the papers tell us about brave boys. Boys who jump into an icy pond to save a friend who has fallen in. Boys who will dash through a fire to save a baby sister. Boys who will stand up against bigger boys who are bullying at school.

Somehow in almost every boy there is a quality of bravery which rises up within him in the moment of emergency.

Look at the little chap in the picture. His father was a cavalier in the days of the great civil war in England. The Roundheads have captured the father's castle and are searching for the father himself. They are very anxious to find him as he is an important man and his capture will mean much to them.

Everyone in the castle is questioned as to the knight's whereabouts, but no one seems to know. Then one of the soldiers has a bright idea. "Ask the children," he suggests. "If they know, they will surely tell."

So the two children are sent for. They are terribly

Bryan with President Hoover.

© Topical

frightened, and the poor mother is even more afraid, for she does not know what the children will say in such an ordeal. But the boy is very brave.

The soldiers ask him, "And when did you last see your father?" But he will not reply. Nothing will persuade him to betray his daddy. How proud his mother must have been that day!

But boys can be as brave to-day as ever they were in the days of old.

Not many months ago, over in the Rocky Mountains of North America, a bus load of happy children left their school one morning and started on their homeward journey. It was winter time and snow was falling. They had not gone more than a few miles when the bus became stuck in a snow-drift and would not move either forward or backward.

Just then a terrible blizzard descended from the mountains and the bus was soon enveloped in snow. The driver did his best to keep the children warm. At first he got them to tear up all their school books and note-books and with these he made a fire in a tin can, round which they crowded for warmth. When all the books were gone they broke up the wooden seats and fed the fire with these.

At last the fire went out, and the driver tried to keep the children warm by getting them to box and wrestle, sing and dance. They managed to keep themselves alive all through the afternoon, evening, and night, until the morning; but then they found that one poor little girl had died.

At this the brave driver decided to go out and search for help. But the snow was so deep and the blizzard so fierce that he lost his way, fell in the snow, and died.

Now before he left the bus he had told one of the older boys, Bryan Untiedt, that he must take charge and keep the children awake at all costs. Bryan was only thirteen at the time, but he rose to the occasion and showed a heroism that stirred the world.

The children were now all huddled together at the back of the omnibus. Suddenly it was noticed that yet another one had died of the awful cold. This made the children frantic and in the excitement one of them broke a window and thus left them quite open to the wind and snow. Bryan tried to keep up their spirits and started the boxing and wrestling again. But they were all getting exhausted now, and could not keep it up for long.

Noticing that his own little brother had become unconscious, this dear brave lad actually took off all his own clothes, save only his underclothes, and wrapped them around his brother. But the little brother died also and then they all, one by one, fell down on the floor of the bus and lost consciousness.

It was not until late that afternoon that a farmer stumbled accidentally upon the bus. He was horrified to find the heap of unconscious children inside and as fast as he could he carried them to his home. Many did not recover, but Bryan was soon well again. For his bravery he was sent for by President Hoover, an honour he well deserved.

All brave deeds are not noticed and written about in the papers as this one. Many are done out of sight and only God sees them. Yet some of these are the bravest of all.

It is a brave deed to speak the truth when it may bring us suffering. When teacher asks at school, "Who has been talking while I've been out of the room?" it is a brave deed to hold up your hand and say, "I did, sir."

The teacher may look very solemnly at you and tell you to stay in for half an hour after school, but in his heart he will admire you for your honesty and courage.

It is a brave deed to resist a temptation to do wrong. When someone would lead you to steal or to lie or to swear and you say, "I cannot do that," you have done a very noble deed that takes more courage sometimes than jumping into a river to rescue a drowning friend.

And it is a brave deed to break away from a com-

Sylvia I. Venus

© S.W.P.

It's a brave boy who gets up directly Mother calls!

panion whom you know is leading you downhill. It is sometimes a very hard thing to do and calls for the highest courage.

It is a brave deed also to refuse to laugh when the laughter would cause suffering to others; or to refuse to laugh at an unholy jest or an impure story. The boy who can turn away at such a time, or better still say, "Stop it boys, this isn't right," is brave indeed.

The world needs more brave boys like these. There is room for them everywhere. They are wanted at school, on the playing field, and in the great battles of after life. God bless them!

Stories

for

Tiny Tots

By Hofmann   © Franz Hanfstaengl

Jesus blessing the bread at Emmaus.

A Page of Blessings

When Jesus lived on the earth, before He would eat bread, He first blessed it. And from this example of the Master has come down to us the beautiful custom of "saying grace" before meals.

I wonder what you say when you "ask the blessing" or "say grace"?

I know one little boy who used to say, very simply, and with his eyes tight shut: "Thank God for this good food, Amen."

That's very brief, isn't it?

When I was in Birmingham once I heard a little girl say this blessing, and I thought it was very beautiful indeed:

"Thank you! for the world so sweet,
Thank you! for the food we eat;
Thank you! for the birds that sing,
Thank you, God, for ev'rything."

One that children often say is this:

"For what we are about to receive may the Lord make us truly thankful, Amen."

You may have said that very often, but if you think a little more what the words mean, perhaps you won't say it so fast as you have done.

Here is another beautiful little blessing:

"Bless this food which now we take
And make us good for Jesu's sake.
                    Amen."

And here is yet another:

"Dear Jesus as our heads we bow,
For this good food we thank Thee now,
                    Amen."

And if you do not wish to say your blessing in poetry, you can say this:

"We thank Thee, dear Lord, for this good food. Bless us now. Make us strong for Thy service. Remember the poor and needy. For Jesus' sake, Amen."

And now you won't forget to say your blessing next meal time, will you?

"Unto Seventy Times Seven"

You will remember that it says in the Bible that we should forgive our brothers when they annoy us "seventy times seven."

That sounds a terrible lot of times. If only the Bible had said seven times it would have given us a chance to be cross now and then, wouldn't it? But seventy times seven! Dear me! That is four hundred and ninety times!

I am sure Jesus made it all that number so that we should lose count and so go on forgiving all the time.

Well, I saw a beautiful illustration of this the other day. There were two boys in it. So that you won't know who they really are I will just call them Tom and Tiny.

Tom was the big brother and Tiny the little brother.

Now Tom was a big tease. Nothing pleased him more than to worry his little brother until he was well-nigh frantic. He would tread on Tiny's train lines, tip the engine over, tilt the signal down when Tiny wanted it up, block up the tunnel just as Tiny was sending the engine through it. They were all very little things, but they just made poor Tiny mad.

In desperation Tiny left his trains and started to paint in his new paint-book. Tom poked his arm and

69

the brush made a nasty smudge right across the page. Poor Tiny! It seemed as though he couldn't get peace to do anything.

They went into the garden. Tiny got on to his tricycle. Before he had gone two yards Tom jumped in front so that Tiny couldn't move another inch. Tiny backed and started off in another direction, but still teasing Tom stood in the way.

"Oh Tom, do stop it!" cried poor little Tiny, getting fairly desperate.

But Tom took no notice. The more agitated Tiny became the more he seemed to enjoy the fun.

"Do get out of my way!" cried Tiny again. "You are just a horrid boy, Tom, and I'll never love you any more."

Just then a voice called from the kitchen. Tiny ran indoors.

"I've brought you something nice back from town," said Mamma.

"Have you, what is it?" asked Tiny, all excited.

Mamma opened her bag and brought out a bar of chocolate cream. "What do you say for that?"

Like a flash Tiny's arms were round Mamma's neck. "Thank you lots and lots," he said.

As he turned to go back to the garden he stopped and looked round.

"And some for Tom, too," he said.

From the depths of Mamma's bag came another bar and Tiny ran off happily to find his brother.

"Some for Tom, too." Dear loving little heart! All the teasing forgotten and forgiven so soon!

What a lesson for us all!

Paul's Lesson

Paul's great ambition in life at the moment was to make a sailing boat. He had found a piece of wood about two feet long and six inches square and was proceeding to hollow it out with a mallet and a chisel.

If you have never done this, you have missed one of the joys of life. At any rate, Paul enjoyed it. He became so interested that he could think of nothing else. As soon as he returned from school every evening he would rush off to his little workshop and start on his job again.

Gradually the piece of wood took shape. Little by little, chip by chip, the hole became deeper and deeper. There was not much left to do now and soon he would be able to nail on the deck and start to work on the mast and sails.

Then came the Sabbath. From his earliest years Paul had learned that this was a day to be kept holy. He had been to church on this day as far back as he could remember. Ordinary work was always laid aside. He kept his very best books to read on this day. To all the family it was a time of rest and peace.

This week, however, the Sabbath seemed to Paul to have come at the wrong time. More than anything else he wanted to finish his boat. There were only a few days left before the holidays, and he feared that he would not have it ready in time. If only he could work just a little while longer he would be able to finish hollowing out the hull at least.

In the morning he went to church as usual. In the afternoon, however, he told Mother that he would rather not go out for the usual walk. He would look after the house while Mother went out, he said.

Mother had not gone long, however, before Paul closed the book he was reading and got up out of his chair. He knew that he had not followed a line of the book. All the time he had been thinking about the boat. Something seemed to be shouting in his ears, "Boat, boat, boat!"

He wandered about the house for a little while, still uncertain what to do. Very faintly another voice said to him, "Remember the Sabbath day, to keep it holy."

Then the first voice started again, "Boat, boat, boat!"

Gradually Paul moved towards his workshop. He opened the door and looked in. There could be no harm in looking in, of course, even on the Sabbath day, he told himself.

Yes, there was the boat, just as he had left it the evening before, almost finished. Another half an hour's work, thought Paul, and the hull would be ready for the deck. What a pity to have to wait another whole day before he could touch it!

He went in, shut the door behind him, and walked over to the boat. Admiringly he stroked his hand over the smooth surface of the wood.

Then, before he quite realized what he was doing, he had picked up the mallet and given one bang to the chisel. The noise resounded through the stillness of the house and made Paul just a little frightened. He looked round to make sure the door was shut.

Bang! He gave the chisel another hit.

Again he felt afraid. Would Mother hear? Whatever would she think of him? But there, Mother was bound to be out for another half an hour. She always did go out for an hour's walk on Sabbath afternoons.

Bang! out flew another chip of wood.

Paul became bolder. Every hit became a little harder. But he was still very nervous.

"Oh!" he cried, all of a sudden. The mallet had missed the top of the chisel and had come down on his thumbnail.

Tears filled his eyes and he danced round the room for a minute until the pain had eased. He began to wonder whether he should have stayed, but now there was only such a little bit left to do he thought he might as well finish it.

"Bang!"

"Oh!" cried Paul in dismay. This time he had hit the chisel a little too hard and it had gone right through the boat. His beautiful work was spoiled. He could have wept, for now it would be so difficult to make the boat watertight.

He was almost persuaded to stop, but the misfortune had made him desperate.

Bang! Bang! Bang! He hammered away faster than ever, very fearful now that Mother might return any minute and find him there.

"Oh!"

The chisel had slipped and cut his hand. It was a bad cut, and Paul knew it. He wrapped his handkerchief around it and ran from the room.

"Mother, Mother!" he cried, "I've cut myself badly. Mother, where are you?"

Fortunately Mother was nearing home. She heard Paul's screams some distance away and came running to him as fast as she could.

As Mother entered the front door Paul fell over in a faint, and it was some time before he was well enough to explain what had happened.

When he opened his eyes again he found himself sitting in one of the arm-chairs in the dining-room. Mother was bathing his forehead with cold water.

Paul began to stare at something on the wall.

"What's the matter, dearie?" said Mother, soothingly. "Don't look so worried."

"Look," said Paul, "fancy that being in front of me now."

"What?" asked Mother, very puzzled.

"That!" said Paul.

Mother looked and at last began to understand. For there she read the old familiar words:

"A Sabbath well spent
   Brings a week of content
   And strength for the tasks of the morrow;
   But a Sabbath profaned
   Whate'er may be gained
   Is a certain forerunner of sorrow."

When Daddy Phoned Up

Master John was the idol of his daddy's heart. Everything that Master John did was perfectly right —to Daddy.

Mamma would sometimes tell Daddy at night-time about some of the mischief Master John had been up to during the day. But Daddy would say, without the least sympathy for Mamma, "Poor little dear, he had to amuse himself somehow, didn't he?"

Even when Master John had wiped his coal-black fingers all over Mamma's newly-washed clothes, all that Daddy said was, "Ah, but he's a bright boy; he must have known those clothes were clean or he wouldn't have done it."

But one day Daddy had a little experience for himself.

He was up in London and in a terrible hurry to get an important document which he thought he had left at home. In a frenzy of anxiety lest after all he might have lost it on the way up in the train, he went to a telephone box and called up his home.

At last he was put through. And this is what happened next.

"Is that Henford 4242?"

"Yaaaaaaaa."

"I say, is that Henford 4242?"

"Heeeeeeee."

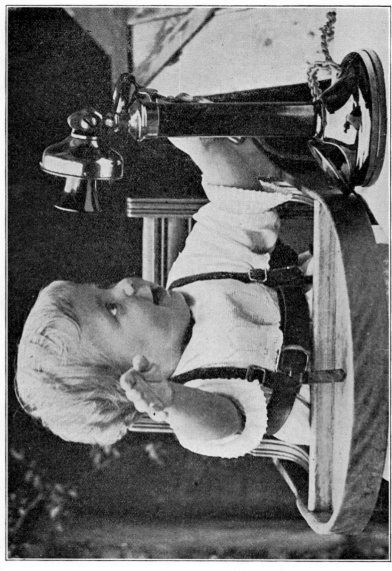

When Daddy phoned up.

© Fox Photos

"There's something wrong with the phone. Is that you, Maggie?"

"Dad-dad-dad-dad-dad-dad."

"What is the matter? I want that document I left on the hall table this morning."

"Goo-goo-goo-goo-goo-goo."

"Can't you understand what I say? I've lost that document. At least I haven't got it. Is it at home? Can't you hear me? Is that Henford 4242?"

"Dad-dad-dad-dad-dad-dad."

Daddy rang off in a towering rage.

When he reached home that night he demanded an explanation. Something had got to be done about it. He could not afford to waste good money like that on telephone calls. And when he did call, why did not someone answer him in an intelligent way? Whoever dared to say all that gibberish when he was anxiously awaiting news of an important document? And so on.

Mamma waited until it was all over. Then she burst into peals of laughter.

"I came in just as you rang off," she said at last, "and what did I find but Master John trying to talk into the phone with the ear-piece held up as though he had used it for years."

"Well!" exclaimed Daddy. "So it was Master John, was it? A remarkable boy, my dear. I always did say he was a most intelligent child. I must go up and kiss him for that right now, even if he is asleep."

"Well, I never did!" said Mamma, as Daddy bounded upstairs.

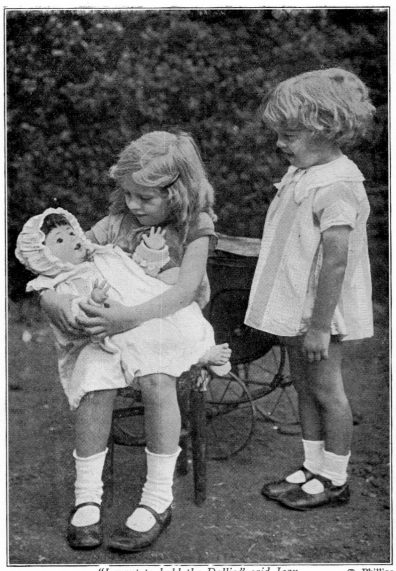

"*I want to hold the Dollie,*" *said Jean.* © Phillips

The Strange Fate of Matilda

It was Dorothy's birthday. The postman had brought a wonderful brown paper parcel and Mother had put it on Dorothy's chair at the breakfast table.

When Dorothy came into the dining-room her eyes opened so wide Mother thought they would never shut again. She rushed across the room and started to open the parcel at once. Off came the string and the paper and the lid and then——

"What a lovely dollie!" she cried. "How good of Uncle. He knew just the very thing I wanted. Isn't she a perfect beauty? I believe she even has a wax face. I am going to call her Matilda, and I'm sure I shall love her for ever and ever!"

Just then Little Sister came running into the room.

"What a booful dollie," she cried. "Do let me hold it just a minute."

"Oh no, indeed," said Dorothy. "You must never touch Matilda. I will let you look at her sometimes, but mind, you must always leave her alone."

"I want to hold the dollie," cried Jean, stretching out her little arms. "I won't hurt it."

"Get away," said Dorothy angrily. "You must not touch her."

Jean turned away, but there were tears in her eyes. A little later she came back to Dorothy, who was still hugging the dollie, and begged to be allowed to hold it "just for a minute."

"No," said Dorothy. "You may look at her, but you must not touch her. You might break her head, and then what should I do?"

Jean followed Dorothy around all the morning, begging for Matilda. Dorothy went into the garden and put Matilda into her dollie's pram. Still Jean begged.

"I want to hold the dollie," she cried. "I won't hurt it."

"You are not going to hold Matilda," said Dorothy. "She's mine, and I don't want her broken."

"You are a mean girl," said Jean, tears rolling down her cheeks. "I only want to hold her just a minute."

"Do leave me alone," said Dorothy. "I want to enjoy Matilda all by myself."

But still Jean begged and begged. At last Dorothy rushed indoors and upstairs, Matilda in her arms. Opening a cupboard door she pushed Matilda inside, intending to keep her out of sight till Jean should have forgotten about her.

Jean was waiting for her at the bottom of the stairs. "Where's that dollie?" she asked. "Do let me hold her just a minute."

"I won't," said Dorothy. "She's gone, anyway."

And so she had, too.

If only Dorothy hadn't been so bad-tempered she would have noticed which cupboard it was in which she had put Matilda to sleep. But being so very angry she had failed to see that it was the cupboard which had the hot-water tank in it. Consequently the longer

Matilda lay there the warmer she became. And after a while little tears of wax began to roll down her cheeks. By and by she had no nose left at all and her eyebrows had fallen off.

When at last Dorothy opened the cupboard door again it was a sorry sight indeed that met her eyes. What she said and what she did had better be left unrecorded. But as she wept and wailed one thought kept coming to her mind, "If only I had let Jean hold her this would never have happened!"

And all her life she never forgot this lesson, that things that are shared often last longer than those one tries to enjoy alone.

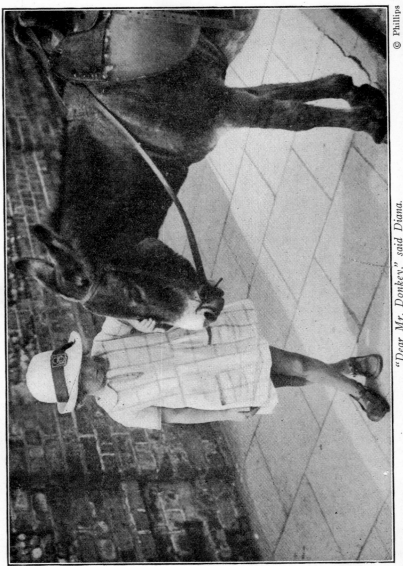

© Phillips

"Dear Mr. Donkey," said Diana.

Diana's Donkey Ride

"Do let me have a ride on a donkey," begged Diana for the five hundred and fifty-fifth time that afternoon.

"No," said Mamma. "I've told you, Diana, that you cannot have anything else to-day. You want everything you see, and if there's a new way to spend money you find it. So please don't let me hear anything more about that donkey business."

"But Mamma——" pleaded Diana.

"No!" said Mother.

Diana walked away. Evidently, she thought, it was no use worrying Mother any more. She strolled away towards the donkeys.

There were a dozen of them, all standing together, waiting for children to come and ride on them. Even while Diana watched, a group of children came up, paid their pennies to the man in charge, and went off gaily along the sands.

There was only one donkey left, and he stood there, good as gold, even though his master had gone away. Diana went up to him and stroked his nose.

"Dear Mr. Donkey," she said, "you'd like to give me a ride, wouldn't you, if I had enough pennies?"

"Hee-haw," said the donkey.

"You are a dear," said Diana. "I believe I could ride you all by myself. It must be easy. Look at all those other children."

As Diana looked at the other children she realized that both they and the man in charge of them were

a long way off and that she was alone with this donkey.

At once a great idea came into her mind. She
would have a little ride after all, even if she only just
sat on his back and moved around in a circle. Surely
the man wouldn't want any pennies for that.

Nearby were some steps on which the children
stood when getting up on to the donkeys' backs. Very
cautiously Diana led her donkey over to them and
climbed up. Nobody seemed to notice her and she
felt very pleased with herself.

As for the donkey he seemed quite used to this
sort of thing and stood there docile as a lamb. Diana
was delighted. She was on a donkey at last, even
though Mamma hadn't given her any money for it.

Suddenly, however, something happened to Mr.
Donkey. He seemed to realize that he had been left
behind by the others. While he had been standing
alone, it had not mattered, but now that he had someone on his back he felt that he should be with his
friends. So, turning round, he jogged off at a smart
pace across the sands.

Diana was never more frightened in her life. What
would the man say? She had no pennies to pay him.
And what would Mamma say when she found out?

Gladly would she have jumped off, but she dared
not. She took hold of the reins, but the donkey only
moved the faster.

Donkeys do not usually run very fast, but to Diana
this one seemed to be rushing away with her at a
terrible speed. He seemed to hear the others in the
distance and wanted to catch them up.

Bump, bump, bump, bumperty, bump! On went

the donkey, with Diana rolling from side to side, expecting to fall off any moment and almost panic-stricken with fear.

"Stop Donkey, stop Donkey!" she gasped.

But Mr. Donkey had no intention of stopping just yet.

"Oh, why didn't I do what Mamma said!" thought Diana. "This is terrible. Won't he ever stop?"

Bump, bump, bump, on across the sands, over the breakwaters, went the donkey.

Why, who was that? Mamma, of course. The donkey was taking her past the very place where she was sitting quietly knitting in her deck chair.

"Mamma!" shrieked Diana.

Mamma looked up from her knitting. In an instant she took in the situation and started running after Diana.

"Stop that donkey!" she cried. "Stop that donkey!"

Other people heard her cry and saw her running. They took up the chase as well. Presently there were more than a dozen people rushing along the sands behind the donkey. As for him, he thought it was one huge joke and ran faster than he had ever done in his life.

Poor Diana! What she suffered! She felt sure she would never be able to sit down again all her life.

By this time the other donkeys had reached the end of their course and turned back. The driver soon saw what had happened. He came running towards Diana.

"Hi, hi!" he called out, very angrily.   "What does this mean?"

But Diana did not care what it meant.

"Take me off, take me off," she cried.

He took her off and told her some things she will not forget for some time.

And after Mamma had paid the driver what he asked for Diana's ride, she also told her some things which she will not forget for some time.

And every time Diana sat down during the next two weeks she remembered her sins and passed a new resolution never to disobey Mamma again.

While Mamma Was Out

"Mamma must go out for just a little while. Baby will be a good boy, won't he?"

"Yes," said Baby, as though anything else was quite impossible.

"And Baby won't try to get out of his chair?"

"No," said Baby, as though he would never dream of attempting anything of the kind.

"And Baby won't touch anything on the table?"

"No," said Baby very solemnly, but casting his eyes over everything on it, nevertheless.

"And Baby won't do anything naughty at all," said Mamma, as though to cover all possibilities.

"No," said Baby, with a smile that was brimful of mischief. "Baby be very good."

"Mamma will come back ever so quickly. By-by, darling. Mamma's only going down the garden."

"By-by, Mamma."

For a moment or two His Majesty was content to bang his spoon on the arm of his chair. It made a nice loud noise. But, alas, the spoon slipped from his fingers and went clattering on the floor.

There was nothing else for it but to find something else interesting. The table seemed to provide a source of attraction. But everything had been moved rather a long way off. It was too bad, thought Baby. Why should big people move things so far away when they go out?

But there was a way out of the difficulty. He could

"Baby smiled a smile of perfect innocence." © Fox Photos

at least reach the tablecloth, and he found that by pulling this towards him the things he wanted came too. Unfortunately some of them, including knives, forks, spoons, plates, cups, and saucers, came towards him quicker than he had intended and went over the edge of the table to keep company with the spoon on the floor. They made a perfectly wonderful noise as they fell and Baby chuckled with great glee.

As the tablecloth kept coming towards him so more and more things fell over the side. Each one made a different sound. It was just lovely.

Coming towards him now was a large pot of something. It looked red inside. He caught it just in time and managed to lift it over on to his chair.

What could this be? It looked nice. In went one chubby finger. Ah! lovely, he thought. In went a hand. Then in went the other hand. Before long he had swallowed quite a lot of strawberry jam. What he did not swallow stuck to him in various places. He was just going to dip into it again when the door opened and in walked Mamma.

"Baby!" she cried. "You naughty boy. Whatever have you been doing?"

Baby smiled a smile of perfect innocence.

"Baby sorry," he said.

"Sorry!" exclaimed Mamma going down on her knees to pick up the broken china. "I should think you ought to be sorry, my boy."

We draw a veil over what happened next. Suffice it to say that Baby had his first lesson in the value of obedience.

Jesus the Good Shepherd. © Autotype Fine Art Co.

Kind People in the Bible

When a little boy at school opens his bag of sweets and says to you, "Please take one," you like him very much, don't you? And when you get home you tell Mamma that you met a very kind boy to-day.

Everybody loves kind people, and if you want to be loved by everybody you must learn how to show kindness to others all the time.

Let me tell you where you can meet some kind people you may not have seen before. They live in those wonderful old stories we read about in the Bible.

Once there dwelt together an old man and his nephew. They occupied quite a lot of land with their cattle and the young man wanted to divide it. So the old man said to him, "Choose which you would like. If you will take the left hand then I will go to the right." That was a very kind thing for the old man to say. And yet when the nephew took the very best piece of land for himself the old man was just as kind. He kept his word and went in the opposite direction. That generous old man was Abraham.

Later on in his life three strangers came to his house one day. He had never seen them before and had no idea who they were, but at once he begged them to come in and make themselves at home. He gave orders to his servants to bring them the very best food he had, and would not let them go until they were rested and refreshed. He must have been a very good man to have been so kind to strangers, for it was not until afterwards that he discovered that he had entertained angels unawares.

Now we come to a kind woman. You remember the story of the two spies? Joshua sent them into the city of Jericho, and while they were there someone recognized them as foreigners. They were in deadly peril. But Rahab, the inn-keeper, took them on to the roof of her house and covered them over with straw so that they should not be found. If the soldiers had discovered the spies both they and Rahab would have been put to death. But they did not see them, and at night this kind woman let the two men down over the wall through a window in her house.

Another kind soul we meet in the Bible is the one who gave up her last crust of bread to Elijah. The prophet was very hungry and came to the widow's home seeking food. She had nothing left for herself and her son but a little flour and oil. She was very poor, and as there was a famine in the land there was no way of getting any more food. But she did not think of that. Gladly she made a little cake with the flour and oil and gave it to the hungry man at her door. That was kindness indeed, but she was rewarded for it. The prophet assured her that she would never want for food till the famine was over. And after that, every time she went to the barrel of meal, there was something in it, and her cruse of oil never ran dry. What a good time the angels must have had filling them up every night!

Yet another kind woman meets us in the story of those early days. This one was quite well-to-do. She owned a nice house. But her money did not make her proud or hard-hearted. When she came to know

Elisha and learned that he travelled a good deal up and down the country, she set apart one of her rooms for him and entertained him every time he passed that way. It was very kind and thoughtful of her and Elisha appreciated it ever so much. She, too, was rewarded. Her greatest desire was to have a little son all her own, and because of her kindness of heart God gave her a baby boy.

And now I want to tell you of a very kind black man. He was a friend of Jeremiah the prophet. Now when Jeremiah was put in prison by the king, this black man, who was a servant in the court, was very sorry. Probably Jeremiah had been kind to him one day. Anyhow, when he heard that Jeremiah had not only been put in prison but had also been dropped down into a horrible dungeon, he actually went in to see the king and asked him to take him out of this terrible place at once. The king agreed and sent thirty men with him to see that it was done. They came to the pit and let down a rope to poor Jeremiah so that they could haul him out.

Just then this kind black man showed himself kinder still. He threw some old rags down the pit and called to Jeremiah to put them under his arms so that the rope would not hurt him as the men pulled him up to the surface. Wasn't that thoughtful of him? By the way, his name was Ebed-melech, and the story of his kindness is told in the thirty-eighth chapter of Jeremiah.

Now we come to the story of a very kind boy. We do not know his name, but he was Paul's nephew. One day when Paul was in Jerusalem the people became very excited, and those who did not like him said they would kill him. To protect him the captain of the soldiers took him into the castle. But the wicked people laid a plot to take Paul's life. Forty of them said that they would eat nothing until they had done so. Somehow the news of the plot reached Paul's nephew. Immediately he rushed to the castle and asked to see the captain. He was taken in and the soldiers were very kind to him. On hearing of the plot the captain arranged for Paul to be sent out of the city that very night and so his life was saved by the kindness and bravery of his sister's son.

But who was the kindest of all? Surely you know. Yes, Jesus Himself. He came down to this earth to show people how kind they always should be to one another. So we see Him healing the sick, opening the eyes of the blind, making the deaf to hear and the dumb to speak. We hear Him cheering the poor, comforting the sad, and telling everybody to be more loving and friendly.

Especially was He kind to little children. He loved them best of all. And when the big people told them to go away and be quiet He said, "Suffer the little children to come unto Me, and forbid them not: for of such is the kingdom of heaven."

Nobody could make Jesus unkind. He had many enemies. They were very cruel to Him. But He never said one unkind thing about them. Indeed, even when they had crucified Him, and He was dying there in fearful agony on the cross, He prayed that they might be forgiven. "Father," He said, "forgive them, for they know not what they do."

Shall we ask Jesus just now to make us as kind as that?

The Tearless Land

I suppose everybody cries sometimes. Little boys cry when they are spanked and little girls cry when they are disappointed. Even mothers and fathers cry now and then, I believe, when they are very, very upset.

But some day nobody will ever cry again. It seems almost too good to be true, but it is really so. There is a tearless land where everyone will be supremely happy. Sweet smiles and joyous laughter will light up their faces every moment, and nothing will dim their happiness through the eternal years,

Jesus Himself tells us about this glorious country. "In My Father's house," He says, "are many mansions: . . . I go to prepare a place for you. And if I go and prepare a place for you, I will come again, and receive you unto Myself; that where I am, there ye may be also." John 14:1-3.

A home prepared by Jesus! Can you imagine any tears there? Can you picture anyone weeping in His presence? No indeed! Nobody cries where Jesus is. It is His supreme joy to make people happy. Where He is all tears are forgotten.

And here is another picture of that lovely land: "I saw a new heaven and a new earth," . . . writes John the apostle, "and I saw the holy city, new Jerusalem, coming down from God out of heaven. . . . And God shall wipe away all tears from their eyes; and there shall be no more death, neither sorrow, nor crying, neither shall there be any more pain: for the former things have passed away." Rev. 21:1-4.

I want you to notice that it does not say that we will wipe our own tears away, or that Mother will wipe them away for us, but that God will wipe them away. Could you think of anything more beautiful? The great, the infinite, the almighty God, Creator of the heavens and the earth, He—He will wipe all tears away!

And once He has wiped them away they will never flow again. In that tearless land there shall be no more sorrow, crying, pain, nor death. Nothing to make us want to cry again. For ever and ever we shall feel radiantly happy. No more quarrels, no more disappointments, no more partings, no more saying good-bye.

What a wonderful home it is that Jesus has prepared for us! Surely we must be ready when He comes to take us there. There is not long to wait now. Let us give our little hearts to Him to-day.

Note.—The Companion Volumes to this book, "Bedtime Stories" (First, Second, Third, Fourth, Fifth, Sixth, and Seventh Series), can be obtained at 1/- each, or any five numbers for 4/- from the printers and publishers:

The Stanborough Press Ltd., Watford, Herts.

281/8/32

UNCLE ARTHUR'S
BEDTIME STORIES
(NINTH SERIES)

With Every Good Wish

To ....

From ....

By Rudolph Blind   © Autotype Fine Art Co., Ltd.

Love Divine.

Uncle Arthur's
BEDTIME STORIES
(Ninth Series)

By ARTHUR S. MAXWELL

"Then Jesus beholding him loved him." Mark 10:21.

Registered at Stationers' Hall by
THE STANBOROUGH PRESS LTD.,
WATFORD, HERTS.

CONTENTS

PREFACE

THE ninth series! Whoever would have thought it in 1924 when the first series was sent forth on its mission to the children of the world? I well remember the feeble faith of certain friends when the little enterprise was launched. But instead of being, as some kindly suggested, a "nine days' wonder," it has lasted nine years so far, and there seems to be no stopping. I am afraid I have lost count of the number sold in all parts of the world. The last figure I heard was three millions.

I would like to say again how much I appreciate the kind letters that I constantly receive from boys and girls in many lands about the stories. I endeavour to reply personally to each one, but lest any be missed I take this opportunity to thank you all.

And now we send number nine on its way. Again we have endeavoured to keep to our original purpose of telling stories that are based on fact and true to life, with the object of inculcating lessons of the highest moral value. That this volume also may prove to be a source of blessing both to children and parents everywhere is the earnest prayer of

THE AUTHOR.

Copyright 1932
The Stanborough Press Ltd.,
Watford, Herts.

Caught by the tide—but on a happier occasion. Uncle Arthur and his three sons on holiday.

Caught by the Tide
My Most Exciting Adventure

I HAVE told so many stories about all sorts of boys and girls that perhaps it is time I told one about myself.

In my Bible, beside a certain text, are written three words—"North Uist Ford"—and every time I look at them they bring back to my mind the most exciting experience it has ever been my lot to pass through.

Many years ago—I won't tell you how many— when I was fifteen years old, I decided to go to a missionary college, and in order to obtain the necessary money I arranged with a certain publishing house— the very one that has since printed over a million copies of BEDTIME STORIES—to sell their Bible books during the summer.

They didn't seem to worry much about my age, and sent me to the Outer Hebrides, off the west coast of Scotland, where I soon found myself, quite alone, cycling up and down these barren, wind-swept islands, trying my best to interest people in the books I carried with me.

For some weeks I lived in Stornoway, riding out every day right across the island to the villages on the other side. What a weary journey that was—twelve miles without a house in sight, and sometimes rain and wind beating in my face all the way. I travelled

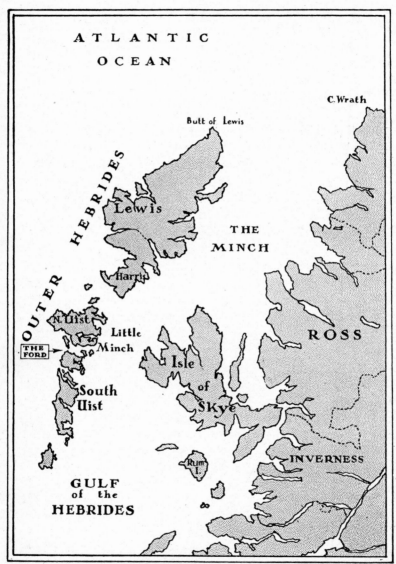

ATLANTIC
OCEAN

C. Wrath

Butt of Lewis

OUTER HEBRIDES

Lewis

THE
MINCH

Harris

N. Uist

THE
FORD

Little
Minch

South
Uist

ROSS

Isle
of
Skye

Rum I.

GULF
of the
HEBRIDES

INVERNESS

The Outer Hebrides—and the ford.

a little farther each day until I had worked right up to the lighthouse at the most northerly point. The lighthouse-keeper, by the way, was very kind. I remember him well, because he bought a book from me!

After doing all I could on the island of Lewis I went by boat down to the next island, called North Uist, and found lodgings in a little thatched cottage, where the rats played round my bed at night. Everything was so primitive that I remember telling my landlady that I didn't think the people were civilized there yet, and, my word, didn't I catch it!

There is a circular road on this island and I cycled and trudged all round it most faithfully, going to places where I am sure no boy of my age had ever tried to sell books before.

At last this island, too, was finished, and I wondered what to do next. So I began to explore southwards, having been given to understand that I could cross to the next large island by walking across the fords at low tide. This appealed to me very much as it would save me the expense of taking the steamer.

Going down to the first ford one morning I looked over it very carefully. The tide was out and from a distance it seemed that all I had to do was to walk straight across the sand to an islet and from there, across more sand, to my destination. But as I drew nearer I realized it was not going to be quite so simple as that. Running through the sand were channels of water, varying, I should say, between ten and twenty feet wide. How deep they were I could not tell. Anyhow, I saw at once that I would have to take my shoes off and wade at least part of the way.

Just then I saw two men begin to cross, and I watched them for some minutes, taking note of the places where they waded through the channels. I noticed, too, that they were hurrying, but did not at the moment understand why. I just thought that perhaps they had some urgent business on the other side. But there was a stronger reason than that.

Taking off my shoes and socks and slinging them around my neck, I began to follow them. Crossing the first channel was simple enough, for I remembered exactly where the men had gone over, and the water was only a few inches deep. But when I reached the second, I was not quite so sure of my position and at my first advance I found that the channel was much deeper than I had expected. I pulled my trousers up above my knees and made another attempt, but could not manage it. Still, however, I was not seriously troubled, and walked up and down the sand till I saw where I could cross in safety.

When I reached the third channel, however, about the middle of the crossing, I confess I began to feel a little uneasy. It was much larger, I noticed, than when I had first looked at it. Even yet the terrible truth had not dawned upon me. Perhaps, if I had been older, I should have understood what a dangerous thing I was attempting, but there, I didn't know, and there was no one to tell me.

By this time I had quite forgotten the place where the men had crossed and had to rely upon making attempts here and there to find shallow water. But this time I could not find it.

Then it dawned upon me that the water was no longer still, as it had been. It was moving, and quite

A typical village street in the Hebrides.   © Topical

rapidly, too. Bits of seaweed, pieces of wood, and sea foam, were floating by. Why, of course, the tide was coming in!

I turned seawards and never shall I forget the sight that met my gaze. Instead of a wide stretch of sand was a vast waste of water. Indeed, it seemed—and the impression will never fade from my mind—that the whole great Atlantic was rolling in upon me.

The island of sand upon which I stood was rapidly becoming smaller and smaller. Every moment the channel beside me was getting deeper and deeper. Within a few minutes the place where I stood would be many feet below the surface of the water. I knew I must act immediately, or be swept away by the fierce, onrushing tide.

But what could I do? If I did not know the way when the channel was shallow, how could I find it now when it had become already twice as deep and was spreading out over the sand in every direction?

Yet somehow, even in that most desperate plight, I felt sure God would see me through. There was no time for long prayers. Every moment was precious. But I remember asking Him to guide me as, taking my courage in both hands, I plunged into the channel.

There was no use trying to save my trousers now. The water came above my knees, above my waist, higher and higher. Would my feet never cease going downwards? For a moment I wondered if I had made a mistake, whether I should not return and try to find my way back through the channels I had crossed. But a glance behind me showed that such a course was now impossible. Everywhere the sand was covered. No one could find the channels now.

Deeper and deeper—was this the end?

Ah! the ground was beginning to rise again. Yes, we must be half-way through! The water was becoming more shallow.

Yet there were other channels still to cross, all

Crofters outside their cottage in the Hebrides.   © Topical

now submerged. How I found my way through them I cannot tell. I can see myself now, with the water above my waist, wandering hither and thither searching with my feet for the shallow places, while all the time I could see the waters from the great Atlantic surging in around me.

Yet I did find my way—or I would not be writing this story now—and at last I crawled out on to the island towards which I had set out so confidently half an hour before. I leave you to imagine my appearance, with all my clothes dripping wet. What a sight I was! If there had been any children around I am sure they would have laughed.

An old man came up to me and told me—just as though I didn't know it!—what a narrow escape I had had. He had been watching me all the time and never expected to see me get over alive. Very kindly he found someone with a boat who took me back to where I had started out and I returned to my lodgings to dry my clothes and thank God for His delivering mercies.

And now you will understand why I have marked that text in my Bible. It is found in the forty-third chapter of Isaiah, the second and third verses. I can't help but feel it was written for me, for this is how it reads:

"When thou passest through the waters, I will be with thee; and through the rivers, they shall not overflow thee: . . . for I am the Lord thy God, the Holy One of Israel, thy Saviour."

Tower Bridge, showing the Tower of London in the distance. The bridge is open to permit ships to pass.

© Topical

What Half an Apple Did

HAVE you heard the story of the horse that held up half—well, nearly half—the traffic of London the other day? No? Then let me tell you about him.

I don't know his name, but let us call him Bill.

Well, Bill started off to work that morning in rather a bad frame of mind. Probably he got out of his stable the wrong side, you know. Anyhow, he was not at all pleased at the thought of having to be harnessed up with Maud to pull a big, heavy lorry from the city to the docks. So he made up his mind to be as troublesome as possible.

When the lorry reached the middle of Tower Bridge, in the very place where vehicles are never allowed to stop, Bill decided he would take a rest. He just stood still and refused to budge.

The carman jumped down and pleaded with him, then threatened him, but all to no effect. Bill simply took no notice. Maud tried to pull alone, but couldn't drag the lorry and Bill, too.

Meanwhile a bus had stopped behind the lorry, and behind the bus two or three cars and another bus. But Bill did not seem the least perturbed. A policeman came up and told the carman to move on, but he replied that he would if he could, but, well, Bill could not be persuaded to take a single step forward.

Then the policeman talked to him, and tried to

drag him forward, but it was no use. Bill was prepared to go to prison rather than move on!

Now the traffic was piling up behind far away into the city, buses, cars, lorries, vans, and motor-cycles, while all the drivers were getting more and more impatient and straining their necks as they tried to peer out to see what all the trouble was about. A tug in the river tooted its syren to say it wanted to get through the bridge, but Bill was supremely indifferent to them all.

About this time a little boy was walking towards the bridge, munching an apple. Seeing the long line of traffic held up he thought there must have been a serious accident. So he hurried on to the place where Bill, now the centre of an interested crowd, was still obstinately standing his ground despite all the entreaties of the carman and the police.

Dick pressed through the crowd to get a better view, still munching his precious apple. Seeing him, the desperate carman suddenly had a bright idea.

"Lend me that bit of apple," he called to the boy.

Dick was taken aback. He didn't want to give up his apple, he was enjoying it too much; but seeing the anxiety on the face of the poor carman, he passed him the half that remained.

The effect was magical. As the carman dangled the apple in front of Bill so he stretched forward to take it. Then he put one foot forward, then the other foot, and before he realized what he was doing he was over the bridge and on his way to the docks again.

Then the buses, the cars, the lorries, the vans, the motor-cycles, the tugs, were all able to move on again

—and all because a little boy had given up half an apple!

What a lot of good that little boy did that morning! He hadn't much to give, it's true, but he gave it willingly, and just when it was needed most. It only shows what little boys can do, if they keep their eyes open for opportunities to help. They may not always be able to do it in such a public way as Dick, but they can be a wonderful blessing sometimes, even at home. Half an apple, a kindly word, a bunch of flowers, or just a little bit of love, sets lots of wheels moving. Try it and see.

"A bunch of flowers."

Red Indians.   © Fox Photos

Love Conquers All

SUCH a noise as there was in the back garden! You never heard anything like it—at least I hope you never did.

Bert and Bob had been playing at Red Indians around the little summer-house at the bottom of the lawn. Bob was dressed up as a chief with feathers he had saved from the chicken run, and Bert was supposed to be trying to keep him from getting into the summer-house.

Then had come the quarrel. Bob said that Bert was dead, because he had shot him with his bow and arrow, but Bert said that he wasn't dead, and wasn't going to be dead for Bob or anybody else.

"You're a cheat," cried Bob, "you are dead."

"I'm not a cheat, and I'm not dead," cried Bert.

"You are."

"I'm not."

"I shan't play any more."

"Don't then, play with yourself."

Both boys got hotter and hotter, and presently Bob hit Bert on the nose. Then there was a tussle, in the midst of which a voice was heard from the dining-room window.

"Come in, come in, both of you," cried Mother. "I will not have this noise in the garden. Whatever will the neighbours think of you?"

Very sullenly the two boys walked towards the house.

"It was his fault," said Bert.

"Wasn't; it was Bert's," said Bob.

"You started it."

"I didn't."

"Never mind, come along, both of you, and sit on these two chairs. And mind, not a sound from either of you for the next quarter of an hour."

Bob and Bert sat down at opposite sides of the room and glared at each other in silence. For when Mother said they were not to talk, she meant it.

Very slowly the minutes ticked away. The boys thought they had never sat still so long in their lives before.

Just before the quarter of an hour was up, Mother came into the room again.

"I'm going to tell you a little story," she said. Their faces brightened.

"Many years ago," began Mother, "when Red Indians used to be as wild and dangerous as Bob seemed to be just now, there used to be terrible fights between them and the white people who were trying to settle in America. The Indians thought that the country belonged to them and that the white people would finally turn them out if they did not fight to retain what was theirs. Many of the white people were very cruel to them, and this only made matters worse.

"Then one day a man landed in America determined to try a different method with the Indians. His name was William Penn, and he thought that he would seek to make friends with them instead of fighting them. He told his people at home that he was going to give them perfect justice and show them all respect and gentleness. Of course, they laughed at him and said that he would be tomahawked and scalped in no time, but he kept to his resolution."

"Didn't he take a gun with him?" asked Bert.

"Your fifteen minutes' silence isn't up yet," said Mother.

"Oh," grunted Bert, subsiding.

"Well, he didn't take a gun with him," Mother went on. "And soon after he arrived in the new country he called all the Red Indians together, as he wanted to talk with them. They came in thousands in all their war paint, and carrying their arms. Probably they suspected a trap. Penn met them with a few friends, all unarmed. Then he talked to them as no white man had ever spoken before. 'We must use no hostile weapons against our fellow-creatures,' he said. 'Good faith and goodwill towards man are our defences. We believe you will deal kindly and justly by us, and we will deal kindly and justly by you. We meet on the broad highway of faith and goodwill; no advantage shall be taken on either side, but all shall be openness and love—for we are all one flesh and blood.'

"After he had finished speaking, Penn pulled out of his pocket a piece of paper on which he had drawn up a treaty to be signed by the Indians and himself. He read it over to them, while they listened with astonishment. This is how part of it read:

"'We will be brethren, my people and your people, as the children of one Father. All the paths shall be open to the Christian and the Indian. The doors of the Christian shall be open to the Indian, and the wigwams of the Indian shall be open to the Christian.'

"It was a very brave thing for him to do, and most of the white people who heard about it said how foolish he was. But the Indian chiefs agreed to the treaty, gave Penn a pledge of good faith, and went away.

"Time went on, and while in other parts of America there was constant fighting, in Pennsylvania —that part of the country was named after Penn— there was peace. When Penn wanted land from the Indians, he bought it at a fair price. If a white man injured an Indian he was punished just the same as if he had injured a white man. Penn also saw to it that the white people did not foist bad goods on the Indians when trading with them. Everybody had to give them fair play."

"And wasn't he ever scalped?" asked Bob, with one eye on the clock.

"No, indeed," said Mother. "The Indians loved him too much for that. And for forty years no un-armed man was killed in the whole state. So you see, by treating the Indians kindly, and never permitting them to be hurt or cheated, he won their friendship and kept peace."

Bob and Bert were fast cooling down now.

"I suppose, then," said Bert, "seeing I am the white man, that I should make peace with that Red Indian over there."

"It would certainly be a very nice thing to do," said Mother.

"Time's up," cried Bob, looking at the clock again. And with happy smiles they both slid off their chairs and ran out happily into the garden.

Ellen's Half-Crown

IT was five o'clock on Christmas morning, just when Dad and Mother were wrapped in deep, happy slumber, that Ellen woke up and felt around in the dark for her stocking.

Yes, it was there, only not so thin and soft as when she had hung it up a few hours before. It bulged here and there, and crackled thrillingly as she touched it.

Ellen got out of bed, switched on the light, unpinned her stocking, and began to examine its contents.

Out came a little box of paints, then a ball, then something wrapped in blue paper, then a tiny box of chocolates, then an orange and an apple. Down in the toe there seemed to be some knobbly things, probably nuts.

Ellen shook the stocking. It jingled. Oh joy! There must be some money there, too! In went her fingers as far as her arm would reach. Out came the nuts and then—a halfpenny. She was a little disappointed, but thought there must be something else because of the chinky noise she had heard.

In went her hand again and this time she pulled out a bright new half-crown that fairly gleamed in the electric light.

"Dad, Mamma!" she cried. "Look what I've

found in my stocking! Wake up and see my lovely half-crown!''

Needless to say, Dad and Mamma were not quite so pleased to be awakened at that early hour as Ellen thought they might be, and it was not long before the light was out again and Ellen lying down wondering why grown-up people wanted to sleep so late on Christmas morning.

When at last they were all downstairs Ellen began to discuss what she would do with her half-crown. In her mind she spent it at least a hundred times, and bought all the things she most wanted. Not being able to decide exactly what she would buy she at last came to the conclusion that she would keep it somewhere safe until she was quite certain.

"I've made up my mind at last," she said to Mamma at tea-time. "I'm going to save my half-crown and open a bank account like Daddy has!"

"Well!" gasped Daddy in surprise. "You are a good girl, Ellen."

"Very thrifty of you," said Mamma, equally surprised. "I will take you down to the post office directly it opens after the holidays and you can then put the money in yourself."

Ellen was charmed at the thought of having a bank account all her own, and waited impatiently for the time when Mamma would be free to take her to town.

At last the day came and off the two went to the post office. There was a very nice lady behind the counter and Ellen thought she liked her very much.

"This little girl," said Mamma, "would like to open a post office account."

"Very good, indeed," said the nice young lady, getting out a little book and picking up her pen.

"Well, dearie, what is your name?" she asked. "And your address?"

Ellen, feeling very important, gave the required particulars.

"And how much do you wish to put in to start the account?"

"Half a crown, please," said Ellen, fumbling for her tiny purse and taking out the precious shiny half-crown.

"Thank you," said the nice young lady, taking it from Ellen and sweeping it, with other money, into the till.

Then a strange thing happened. Ellen began to cry.

At first it was a very little cry, with only one or two tears trickling down her cheeks, but it soon got worse.

"Why Ellen, dear," cried Mamma, "whatever is the matter?"

"Boo-hoo-hoo!" cried Ellen, while the nice young lady wondered what had happened and the other people in the shop looked on and smiled.

"Ellen, Ellen, what is the matter?" cried Mamma, getting alarmed.

"I've lost my half-crown," cried Ellen amid sobs.

"No, you haven't lost it," said Mother. "The young lady has it all right. Don't cry."

"Yes, it is lost, I know it's lost," cried Ellen. "It's all mixed up with all that other money and I shall never see it again. Boo-hoo-hoo!"

At last Mamma had to take Ellen out of the post office and go for a walk with her down the street.

"It's quite all right, darling," she said. "Don't you see, the king has promised to give you your half-crown back again any time you want it. Because of his promise it's just as safe, or safer, than if you had kept it at home. You can go and get it back now if you wish."

Ellen began to see a ray of hope.

"And do you know," went on Mamma, "it's much the same with the kind deeds we do. The angels in heaven keep a record of them. If we give something to the poor, even a cup of cold water, Jesus knows about it. That's how we lay up treasure in heaven. And He, the King of kings, has promised to repay us not only all we put into His bank, but far more besides. He says, 'Give, and it shall be given unto you; good measure, pressed down, and shaken together, and running over, shall men give into your bosom.' And by that He means that He will see to it that we always get back much more than we ever give to Him."

Ellen didn't quite understand all that Mamma tried to tell her, but at least she was comforted over the temporary absence from her little purse of her precious half-crown.

Kenneth's Stockings

TALKING about stockings reminds me of young Kenneth. He had heard the old story about Santa Claus coming round on Christmas eve and, being of a business-like turn of mind, he thought he might as well make the most of the opportunity. If one stocking could be filled in this way, why not many? Surely, especially in the dark, it would be easy to deceive the old man.

Anyway, thought Kenneth, it was worth trying, so he proceeded to hang up all the stockings he could find, Daddy's, Mamma's, Auntie's, Grandma's, Grandpa's, Big Brother's, Big Sister's, and the maid's. Everybody's stockings were, in fact, brought into use and duly pinned on to Kenneth's cot before he went to sleep that night.

"What a lot of things I shall get," he said to himself as he surveyed the long line of suspended hosiery —big socks, little socks, white socks, brown socks, black socks, clean socks, and dirty socks. "If they are all full in the morning, I shall be the happiest boy in the world!"

At last Kenneth fell asleep to dream of his stockings. He saw them all full of the loveliest things. One had a steam engine in it, another a teddy bear, another a big box of chocolates, another a trumpet. They were all so real he could almost feel himself playing with them.

Anticipation. © Topical

About midnight—if only Kenneth could have seen!
—two people crept stealthily upstairs and peered into
his bedroom.

"He's fast asleep," said one. "I think it's all
right."

"Yes," said the other. "Tread very quietly or
you'll wake him up."

"Why look at all these stockings!" exclaimed the
first voice.

"Yes," said the second voice, "he borrowed all
our stockings. He said he wanted to have them all
filled."

"Rather greedy," said the first voice.

"I'm afraid it was," said the second voice.

"Well, we'll have to teach him a little lesson,"
said the first voice.

"But don't be too hard on him," said the second
voice.

"We won't. We will certainly put something into
every one of them. Let's start at this end."

"All right. Do be careful. See, he's getting dis-
turbed."

"You hold the stockings," said the first voice,
"and I'll put the things in."

"All right, be quick," said the second voice.

The two figures worked away rapidly in the dark.

"Pretty steam engine," said Kenneth in his sleep.

"Bless me!" said the first voice. "I thought he
had caught us."

"Oh dear!" exclaimed the second voice. "It gave
me quite a turn."

"Where's the smallest sock?" asked the first
voice.

"Here it is," said the second voice.

"That's the one I've been looking for. Hold it open."

The figures bent over the cot to make sure Kenneth was really asleep, gave him a good-night kiss, and moved quietly out of the room.

Morning arrived. Very early morning, too. In fact the grey light of dawn had scarcely begun to peep through the curtains when Kenneth woke up. In a moment he had thrown off his bedclothes and was standing up in his cot feeling along his row of stockings.

Hurrah! Every stocking had something in it. He had been right after all. They weren't all full, truly, but every one had something at the bottom. Some of them were quite heavy, too. He began to examine them more closely.

Down into the first one went his chubby little arm and out came—a banana!

"Umph!" grunted Kenneth. Not so bad for a start, he thought, but hardly what he had expected. He removed the skin and began to eat it. "Now for the second," he said to himself.

Down, down, down, he went, right into the toe. And this time, out came a ball! He was glad to get the ball but—where was the steam engine?

From the third he brought a little packet of sweets, and from the fourth an orange. Each stocking had just one little thing at the bottom of it, and nothing else. It was rather disappointing. Not till he got to the last —the smallest of all, did he find it full of all sorts of little things he had wanted. But where was the teddy bear? Where was the engine? Where was the trumpet?

It was rather a forlorn little Kenneth who came down to breakfast that morning.

"Hallo, dear!" cried Daddy. "How about all those stockings? Did you find them full?"

"Naw," said Kenneth, rather disgustedly. "He made a mistake."

"A mistake?" cried Daddy. "How's that?"

"Well, he just took one decent stockingful and spread it out among them all. I call that cheating."

"Ha! Ha! Ha!" laughed Daddy. "What a bit of fun! But do you know what I think?"

"What?" asked Kenneth, still rather upset.

"I think that when he saw all those stockings he got a shock and said to himself, I reckon a very greedy boy lives here and I'll teach him a lesson."

"Umph," grunted Kenneth. "I shan't hang them all up next time. I didn't get nearly all I wanted."

"Oh, by the way," said Daddy, "I found a parcel addressed to Kenneth in the hall this morning."

"Did you?" Kenneth's eyes brightened.

"Yes, here it is."

Kenneth seized it with delight and ripped off the paper. Inside were the engine, the trumpet, the teddy bear—and a box of chocolates.

"He must have dropped this parcel on the way upstairs," he said eagerly.

"Ahem, perhaps he did," said Daddy.

Native boys at work on a mission garden.

God's Hands

JERRY was working on his little garden at a mission school in West Africa, when he was suddenly taken ill and had to be removed to the hospital.

This was a great disappointment to him because it was but three weeks before the annual inspection of all the gardens by the superintendent, and Jerry had so hoped to get the prize this year. Every day he had worked his very hardest, digging, planting, weeding, and striving his utmost to make his the best garden on the mission.

But now all his hopes seemed shattered. As he lay in the hospital he pictured the weeds growing up— they grow very quickly in West Africa—and spoiling all that he had done. As inspection day drew nearer, and he was not allowed to get up, he knew that there was no possible hope of his winning now. The other boys would be working hard on their gardens and making them look all spick and span. Of course, he reflected, it wasn't his fault; he had done his best, and he felt sure the superintendent would understand.

But meanwhile something was happening of which Jerry had no knowledge. Daniel, Jerry's friend, had had a bright idea. He, too, was going in for the competition, but he thought it was too bad that Jerry should stand no chance at all because of his illness. He had talked to the other boys about it and they had all agreed to give just a little time each day to keeping the weeds out of Jerry's garden until inspection day came round. So while, of course, they still tried to make their own gardens the best, they gave this little extra bit of care and love to that of the poor sick boy who could not look after his own.

At last inspection day arrived. Jerry was still lying in the hospital, and to-day he was very discouraged. He thought he could see his garden covered with weeds. He pictured the superintendent going round and saying, "Whose is that garden over there with all those dreadful weeds in it?" And then he seemed to hear some of the boys saying, "Oh, that's Jerry's garden."

It was too bad, he thought. Fancy! that it should happen like this after all his work—and he knew he had worked harder than the others. It really didn't seem fair.

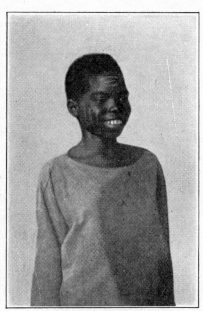

A happy African boy.

Jerry was becoming more and more miserable when suddenly the door of the ward opened and, to his astonishment, in walked the superintendent and a group of the boys. Whatever could this mean?

"We have come to congratulate you," said the superintendent, "on winning the prize for the best kept garden this year."

"Me?" said Jerry, with eyes wide open in surprise.

"Yes, you," said the superintendent.

"But—but—it's all covered with weeds."

"Not when I saw it this morning," said the superintendent.

"But—how—what—?" began Jerry.

"It's all right," said Daniel, with a twinkle in his eye. "We are all delighted that you have won the prize. You see, God didn't let the weeds grow on your garden because you deserved to win; He knew you had worked harder than us all."

"I think that's right," said the superintendent, "but I believe He had some human hands to help Him."

At this all the boys laughed happily and ran out again to their work, while Jerry, overjoyed, dropped a little tear of gladness on his pillow.

Bonfire night.　　　　　　　　　　© Topical

Bonfire Night

IT was the fifth of November. For several weeks the children had been collecting all sorts of rubbish and piling it up in the garden for the great annual celebration of bonfire night. There was now a splendid heap of sticks, weeds, boxes, old newspapers, broken barrels, and the like.

"Say, Daddy, can't we have some fireworks?" implored Jim for the ninety-ninth time that morning.

"I don't think we should spend money on fireworks just now," said Daddy. "As I've told you before—."

"Oh, but, Daddy," chorused the rest, "just a few! A few won't hurt anybody, and it won't seem right without just one or two."

"Oh dear!" sighed Daddy. "I suppose I shall have to get some, after all."

"There's a dear Dad. Some squibs, mind, and Roman candles, and rockets, and—"

"But you said a few!"

"All right, then, we'll leave it to you."

"Well," said Daddy, "if I do get a few it's on the express condition that there shall be no quarrelling about them."

"Oh, that's all right," said all together. "We won't quarrel. We never do!"

"Oh no," said Daddy, "of course you don't. I think I've heard that little story before. We'll wait and see."

At last night fell and the great moment for which all the children had been longing for weeks arrived. But no Daddy appeared, and, of course, there were no fireworks.

"It's too bad of him," said Jim. "He might have brought them."

As the minutes passed and Daddy did not come they all became more and more impatient. At last Jim said he was going to light the fire anyway. He struck a match and in an instant there was a great roar as the flames leapt upward. It was a grand sight, but somehow it wasn't the same without Daddy.

"Why hasn't Daddy come?" asked one, then another, as they all got more and more out of sorts. "Why hasn't he brought the fireworks? Why is he spoiling the whole evening like this?"

The fire was already dying down when someone raised the cry, "Here he is!"

Surely, here was Daddy—who had been delayed at the office on important business—running down the garden with a waste-paper basket full of fireworks in his arms.

But it was a poor welcome he received.

"Why have you come so late?" asked Jim.

"You've spoiled the evening," said another.

"It's too bad," said a third, "they won't be any good now."

"Well!" exclaimed Daddy. "I think I will take them away again!"

"Oh no, don't do that!" cried Jim, seizing one of the Roman candles from the basket in a very rude, bad-tempered way and proceeding to set it alight.

"Jim!" said Daddy firmly, "what did I tell you—"

But Daddy did not finish his sentence. The Roman candle was already alight and throwing up a shower of golden rain followed by green and red stars that soared up into the darkness.

Suddenly there was a loud report.

"Bang!"

But the noise did not come from the Roman candle. Everyone turned to the basket.

Yes, a spark from the candle, which had been placed too near the basket, had fallen upon the fuse of one of the large crackers. But worse was to follow.

Bang! Bang! Bang!

The first explosion had smothered the other crackers with sparks and now it seemed that all were going off at once.

"Turn them out of the basket!" shrieked someone. But it was too late. Quicker than thought a flame had shot up and set basket and all on fire.

What a sight it was! Red fire and green fire mingling together, and stars of various colours leaping into the air and spraying themselves around in all directions.

Crack! crack! crack! went the little squibs, jumping all over the place.

Bang! Bang! Bang! went the larger cannons.

Whizz! went a sky rocket right past Jim's head.

It was all over in less than three minutes and then all that was left was the bottom of the waste-paper basket and a group of very sad and disappointed children.

"Well, it was pretty while it lasted," said Daddy, trying to be cheerful.

"And if you had only come earlier—" began Jim, crossly.

"Yes, and if only you had not been so impatient," said Daddy, "we should have been setting off fireworks now."

It was a sorry little party that now filed up the garden, and Daddy's heart melted at the sight of their tearful faces.

By a strange coincidence he found a spare two-shilling piece at the bottom of his trouser pocket and sent one of the boys hurrying off to the corner shop. So they had "a few" fireworks after all. But the lesson of that evening was not soon forgotten. For whenever any of them was tempted to be cross or impatient after that he thought of that terrible night when the fireworks all went off at once.

The Mysterious Letters

"WELL!" exclaimed Miss Simpkins in the teachers' room one morning. "I never saw such an unruly bunch of youngsters as those Hendersons. They invited me round to tea last night and I did have a time of it. As for their manners at table they were simply awful."

"Poor Mrs. Henderson!" said Miss Dawson. "She certainly has a problem with three like Gladys."

"I should say so," said Miss Simpkins. "And you should have seen them grabbing for their food, each one taking the best of everything, and, my dear, actually eating with their knives!"

"I suppose the poor woman has too much to do," said Miss Dawson.

"Perhaps she has," said Miss Simpkins, "but I think she should try a bit harder to reform their manners. It will be so difficult for them when they grow up."

If only the teachers had known, Mrs. Henderson was trying her very best to reform the manners of her three lively children. She had noticed all their bad behaviour during Miss Simpkins' visit and was deeply distressed about it.

"Whatever will teacher think of you all?" she had said almost before the door had closed upon Miss Simpkins' retreating figure. "I'm thoroughly ashamed of you, yes, all of you! Surely when your

41

teacher is here, Gladys, you could have set a better example. It was simply terrible. And you can take it from me that we shall not have anyone else to tea for a very long time."

"Oh Mamma," said Doris, "I did so want Miss Dawson to come next week."

"Oh dear, no!" exclaimed Mamma. "Not after this. Until you children have learned to behave better in company there is no one coming to tea in this house."

"But if Gladys has Miss Simpkins, surely I can have—" began Doris.

"Not until you have all ceased to be little cannibals," said Mamma.

The subject was dropped, but it did not leave Mamma's mind. What could she do to make her children behave better when strangers came in? They were quite normal at ordinary times, but just as surely as someone came on a visit they became excited, and lost their heads. They seemed to know that Mamma would not reprove them in front of a stranger, and made the most of it.

For several days Mamma thought it over, for she knew she must find some way out of the problem. She could not have the family let down like this. At last one morning she struck a bright idea. All day she worked it over in her mind and when the children came home from school she had it ready for them.

They thought it was a great scheme and agreed to start practising it immediately. Doris was especially enthusiastic as Mamma promised that if they would all fall in with the plan she would agree to Miss Dawson being invited to tea next Wednesday evening.

They all had lots of fun over Mamma's idea during the next few days, and as it seemed to be working beyond her best expectations she gladly agreed to the invitation for Wednesday being sent.

"Now you're in for it," said Miss Simpkins when Miss Dawson showed her the invitation she had received. "I hope you come out of it alive."

"Well, it will at least break the monotony of life," laughed Miss Dawson. "I shall certainly be interested to see what happens."

Wednesday evening arrived. At the appointed time Miss Dawson was welcomed to the Henderson home and sat down at the tea-table. There she found three demure little girls sitting as still as mice.

"Strange!" she thought. "This isn't what I expected to find. Miss Simpkins must have been mistaken."

The meal proceeded. They all talked about the weather, school, games, and other things, and gradually the children became more lively. Doris reached forward with a jammy knife towards the butter.

"How many marks did you get for arithmetic today?" asked Mother. Then, under her breath, "B.K."

"Six," said Doris, blushing just a little, while the jammy knife went back on her plate.

At this moment Mamma caught sight of Beryl, the youngest, about to pour her cocoa into her saucer.

"Oh, Beryl," she said, "would you like to show Miss Dawson that scarf you have knitted for your dolly after tea?" Then, under her breath again, "N.D."

"Yes, Mamma," said Beryl, putting the cup back

in its place and stirring the contents vigorously. "Shall I get it now?"

"No, not yet. Afterwards will do," said Mamma. Then, very quietly again, "M.I.C."

Gladys, who had been eyeing the last piece of bread and butter rather anxiously, now reached forward and took it.

Then the cakes were passed round.

"I hope the weather is fine for the holidays," said Mamma, as the dish went from hand to hand. "Ahem, F.H.B."

At this Beryl, who was in the act of taking a second cake, put it back as carefully as possible, while Doris tittered.

Presently the meal was over and the time came for Miss Dawson to go. She said good-bye to the children in the dining-room and Mamma went with her to the door.

"Really, Mrs. Henderson," said Miss Dawson, "your children are good. I don't think I have ever seen a family so well behaved."

"I'm so glad," said Mrs. Henderson, beaming with pride. "It's nice to get a little appreciation sometimes."

When the teachers met in the morning Miss Dawson went straight over to see Miss Simpkins.

"So you've got back alive," said Miss Simpkins, laughing.

"Yes," replied Miss Dawson. "And I think you must have made a mistake about the Hendersons. I found them all behaving like little angels."

"You don't say so! Whatever can have happened to them?" replied Miss Simpkins.

"I don't know," said Miss Dawson. "I think their mother must have worked some magic spell over them since you were there. Anyhow, they said they were going to invite you again soon."

"Oh, rather," smiled Miss Simpkins.

But they did, and a week or two later she found herself back at the Hendersons again, watching to see whether the report given by Miss Dawson was really true. She was indeed surprised at what she found. There was a startling difference, and she tried her hardest to account for it. Once or twice she heard Mrs. Henderson whisper some mysterious letters which seemed to have a remarkable effect on the usually lively youngsters. She determined to find out what it all meant.

"I must congratulate you," she said to Mrs. Henderson as she was leaving the house. "The children have been so good, haven't they?"

"I'm so glad to hear you say so," said Mamma. "I'm afraid they weren't all they should have been the last time you came."

"Well, perhaps, er—" began Miss Simpkins. "Oh, by the way, Miss Dawson and I would love to know the secret of the magic spell you have cast over them."

"Magic spell?" queried Mamma, smiling.

"Yes, those strange letters, you know."

"Oh, did you hear them?" asked Mamma, surprised, and blushing a little. "Oh, they're very simple. You see, 'B.K.' means 'Use the butter knife,' and 'N.D.' means 'Not done.'"

"Ha! Ha!" laughed Miss Simpkins. "But do tell me what 'F.H.B.' stands for, and 'M.I.C.'"

"Well, that's really a secret. But I'll tell you. 'F.H.B.' means 'Family hold back,' and 'M.I.C.' means 'More in the cupboard.'"

"Well done!" cried Miss Simpkins. "I never would have guessed. What a splendid idea!" And still laughing heartily she said good-bye and walked down to the front gate.

Most polite!

The Quarrel in the Kennels

IT all happened one fine morning at the Kennels in Dovecote Lane.

Cæsar and his son Augustus, usually called Gussy for short, lived in one kennel, while Brutus and his son Anthony, mostly called Tony, lived in the kennel opposite. On the whole they were very good friends, but, like most near relatives, they got out of sorts with each other sometimes.

Gussy and Tony had been having a fine old romp together, as they loved to do whenever they were allowed out, and they had been happy enough until Gussy had suddenly spied a bone that must have been accidentally dropped by the man who came round to feed them.

Gussy rushed for it, followed by Tony.

"It's mine!" cried Gussy. "I saw it first."

But Tony was not going to miss so rich a prize as this. So when Gussy seized one end, he grasped the other. Then began a real tug of war.

"Grrrrrrrr," said Gussy, "leave it alone. It's mine."

"Grrrrrrrr," replied Tony, "it's not yours, we both saw it at once."

"Grrrrrrrr," said Gussy, "drop it, I tell you!"

"Grrrrrrrr," replied Tony, "you drop it!"

Now Tony was just a little stronger than Gussy and presently, with a sudden jerk, he wrenched the

"Ha! Ha! Ha!" laughed Brutus. © Fox Photos

"Don't laugh at me!" said Cæsar.   © Fox Photos

bone out of Gussy's teeth and made off with it.

Gussy followed him and after a short run caught him up. And then wasn't there a rough and tumble fight! Over and over they went, barking and yelping, biting and scratching. By this time all the other dogs had come to the doors of their kennels and were looking on with great interest.

"Go it, Tony!" barked some.

"Keep at it, Gussy!" barked others.

"This shouldn't be allowed," barked a few of the older dogs.

"Keeper! Keeper!" barked one, evidently in great distress.

So great was the noise that the keeper soon came on the scene, and seeing what was happening, separated the two puppies and sent them back to their respective parents.

Tony and Gussy were very crestfallen, for not only had neither of them really won the fight, but they had both lost the bone. So they told their parents all that had happened, each, of course, blaming the other.

Cæsar was very angry about it and the roof of his kennel being open he stood up and glared across at Brutus.

"I wish you would bring up your puppies better," he growled. "Poor Augustus has a deep mark on his ear where your ill-behaved Anthony bit him."

"Ha! Ha! Ha!" laughed Brutus, who always saw the funny side of things. "If you had brought Augustus up better he—"

"Don't be rude, and don't laugh at me, you grrrrrrrr!" said Cæsar.

"Oh there's nothing to laugh at, only your face," said Brutus. "Ha! Ha! Ha!"

"Do you call yourself good-looking?" retorted Cæsar. "If I had a face like yours—"

"You would be well off," interrupted Brutus.

"My word!" returned Cæsar, "if only I were not chained up."

"But you are," laughed Brutus. "And so am I. Isn't that fortunate?"

"Grrrrrrrr!" was all Cæsar could say as he dropped down into his kennel again.

"Hallo!" he said, "where's Augustus? I hope he never plays again with that imp of a puppy over there. Augustus! Augustus! Where are you, Augustus?"

He jumped up on his kennel again and looked around.

"Looking for your distinguished son?" asked Brutus, with a twinkle in his eye.

"I am," said Cæsar importantly.

"Just look down the field," said Brutus.

"Well I never did!" exclaimed Cæsar. "There's no accounting for the ways of youth."

For there in the field were Tony and Gussy contentedly chewing at each end of the bone. Just like all good children they had forgiven and forgotten their quarrel immediately and were happy little friends again. Why hadn't they thought of this way out at first?

© Topical

Health and strength are our most precious possessions.

Counting Their Blessings

"HAVE you heard about the Browns?" asked Tom at the dinner table one day.

"No, what about them?" asked Mother.

"Well, they've got an Austin Seven now."

"That's interesting," said Mother. "I hope they get lots of joy out of it."

"Yes, they get all the good things. I don't think it's fair. We barely have enough to keep body and soul together."

"My dear!" exclaimed Mother. "It's not so bad as that. We have quite a nice little home—"

"And they have a better one, and now they've got a car. Why doesn't Dad get a car?"

"Well, you know why. Maybe he will some day. But really, Tom, you mustn't get so discontented. We have many blessings."

"Have we? I can't see them."

"Oh Tom! You are strong, and have very good health."

"What of that?"

"That's more than Alec Brown has. What's more, you never have an ache or pain, you always have enough to eat, you are not deaf, you have splendid eyesight—"

"What if I have?" said Tom rather sulkily. "Other people have, too, haven't they?"

"Perhaps they have," said Mother, "but I have

53

noticed that on the whole God shares out the blessings pretty evenly. It's often said that the richest people have the worst indigestion."

Tom smiled faintly.

"Let me tell you a story, Tom," Mother went on. "Some time ago a poor blind man came to a mission station in India and asked the doctor if he could do anything to help him see again. He had been blind several years, and he did so want to look out on the world once more.

"Well, the doctor looked at the poor man's eyes and realized that there was practically no hope. However, he said he would attempt an operation if the man were willing to take the risk of permanent blindness if it failed. So eager was the man to regain his sight that he accepted immediately. He was prepared to risk anything in the hope of being able to see again.

"At last the mission doctor was able to perform the operation. It was a very painful one, but the man bore it like a hero. Then he was sent home and waited for days and weeks for his eyes to heal. Ever in his mind was the thought, Would he be able to see when the bandages were removed?

"One day there was a great disturbance at the door of the dispensary.

" 'I want the doctor,' cried the man, upon whom the operation had been performed. 'Take me to the doctor!'

"The doctor left his work and went out to see what all the noise was about. And what a picture he saw!

"At the door was the man upon whom he had performed the operation and by his side were two very plain, ordinary little boys, stark naked.

" 'Look, doctor, look!' cried the man. 'Aren't they the loveliest children? I have come to show them to you for I had never seen them before you gave me back my sight. Aren't they beautiful? Aren't they beautiful?' And the poor man almost danced in his delight.''

"What did the doctor say?" asked Tom.

"Of course he was almost as pleased as the man that the operation had been successful, although he could not be quite so enthusiastic about the two dirty little urchins. But, Tom, don't you see, that poor man didn't realize how great were his blessings until he lost one of them. When his sight was gone he was prepared to give everything he had to regain it. And when, by God's providence and the doctor's skill, he regained his sight, he realized how very beautiful were some of the other ordinary things he had.''

"I think I see what you are getting at," said Tom, with another little smile.

"I am glad you do, dear. After all, Jesus was right when He said that 'a man's life consisteth not in the abundance of the things which he possesseth.' There is a lot of happiness to be found in the very ordinary things we have. We should never grumble about them lest they be taken away and we see how foolish we have been.''

"Dear Mother," said Tom, throwing his arms round her neck. "You are always right. I'll try not to feel discontented any more.''

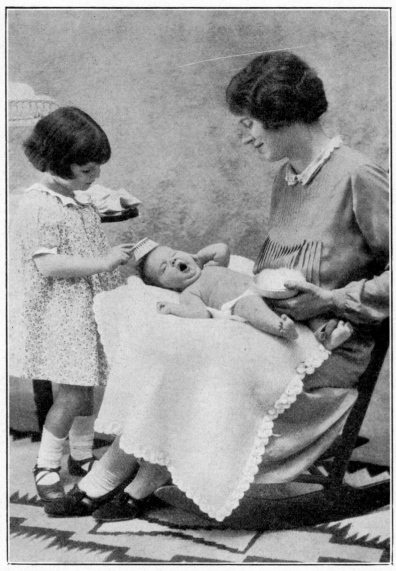

Mother love. © Anne Shriber

Mother Love

HERE is a very sad little story, and I hope you won't shed too many tears as you read it.

Once, not many years ago, there lived on the outskirts of a small Australian town a mother and her baby daughter. They were quite alone in their cottage, for their Daddy had died some time before.

Little Margaret was all this poor mother had left in the world and, as you can imagine, she loved her very dearly.

One evening the mother wanted to do some shopping and, as it was getting late, she decided to put Margaret to bed and go out by herself. She did not like leaving Margaret alone, but it was the only thing to do. There was no one to leave with her.

So Margaret was bathed and put to bed with many good-night kisses, and when she was sound asleep the mother tip-toed out of the room and hurried down to the market.

But alas, she had forgotten to turn out the oil lamp in the sitting-room and shortly after she had left home, the cat, perhaps running across the table after a mouse, knocked the lamp over. Had someone been there to pick it up quickly, all might have been well, but there was no one to help, and poor pussy did not understand.

The oil spread all over the table-cloth and in a few moments it was ablaze. As the cloth burned so it fell in pieces on the floor and set the carpet on fire. Within ten minutes the whole dining-room was burning fiercely.

A neighbour, passing the house, saw the smoke pouring from the window, raised the alarm, and called loudly to the occupants to run out for their lives. But as baby was asleep and Mother was in the market-place no one answered, except the cat, and the neighbour concluded that everybody must be out.

Others were soon on the scene, bringing water from the well and throwing it through the windows upon the flames. By this time the fire had obtained a very strong hold and the friends who had gathered realized that their feeble efforts could do little to help. Even when the village fire brigade arrived and brought up their hose and pump they made no effect upon it. Smoke was pouring out of every window and it looked as though it could only be a matter of minutes before the whole house would be consumed.

Suddenly a piercing cry was heard and a woman was seen rushing through the throng of spectators.

"My baby! My baby!" she cried. "She is upstairs in the front room."

Everyone gasped in horror, for they had thought it was only an empty house that was burning.

The brave little mother made as if to dash into the house, but the firemen ran forward to restrain her. "It's no use now," they said; "no one could live a moment in there."

"Let me go, let me go!" cried the mother, with superhuman strength throwing the men aside.

Then without a thought for her own safety she plunged through the smoke into the raging furnace, dashing up the half-burned stairs into the room where her precious child lay.

The firemen had been right. It was not possible for anyone to live amid such smoke and flames. But the mother reached her baby and when the fire was over they found them both together, the child clasped tightly in her mother's arms.

How wonderful is the love of a mother! Of course, yours would do just the same for you. I know she would. If you were in ever such a dangerous place, Mother would rush to help you out, even though it cost her all she had and her own life as well. Now, wouldn't she? Can you imagine anything Mother wouldn't do for you if you really needed it?

And if that's true, and you know it is, don't you think that while you have the chance you could show her how much you love her, too? I know you would gladly dash into a burning house to save your mother. Of course you would. That would be a grand heroic thing to do. But you need not wait for such a rare opportunity to show your affection. Why not try washing the dishes for her next time she's tired? I'm sure she would appreciate that just as much! Anyway, it's worth trying, isn't it?

At the wicket. © Fox Photos

Three Wickets for a Duck

IT was an exciting match. The sides were: Daddy versus "The Rest." At the close of the first innings the score stood as follows:

Daddy.........25   "The Rest".........25

So they were even. Now they were in the midst of the second innings, and Daddy had just been caught out for one!

What glee! Only two runs to make to win, and three lusty boys to help make them.

Tim took up the bat—he always liked to go in first, when he could—and strode importantly to the wicket.

He turned to face Daddy's bowling with a confident smile. But Daddy was a little desperate, for he knew everything depended now on the way he bowled.

Click! The ball touched the off stump and scattered the bails.

Tim flung his bat on the ground in disgust.

"You bowled too fast," he cried. "You always bowl too fast!" But Tom picked up the bat and went to the wicket.

"Play!" cried Daddy, sending the ball down more slowly this time. It bumped along the ground and Tom rushed out to hit it. He missed and, turning round, saw his middle stump bent backwards.

"Out!" cried Daddy, very pleased with himself.

"It's not fair!" cried Tom. "You bowled me too slowly!"

Daddy laughed. "Next man, please." He was getting excited now. Only one more—there was still a chance of victory, even though he had only made one run himself.

George, the eldest, took up the bat, with a look on his face that said: "I am the hope of the side."

"Now a really nice one for you, sir," said Daddy, smiling, and half expecting the ball to be knocked over the roof of the house.

"Play!"

Down went the ball, rather swiftly, and not very high from the ground. George made a great hit at it and thought he had sent it at least into one of the bedroom windows, but no, he had really missed it. And once more the bails were scattered over the grass.

"Out!" cried Daddy again. "All out for nought! Three wickets for a duck!"

"It's not out! No ball! They were all grounders! It's not fair! We won after all!" cried the three boys.

And what a scene there was! Daddy was dancing a jig on the lawn to celebrate his success and laughing enough to break the buttons off his waistcoat, while "The Rest" were shrieking that they weren't beaten at all, and pulling up the stumps with a vow that they would never play cricket again.

The debate continued for some hours. When "The Rest" had gone to bed that night, Daddy went to the bottom of the stairs and called out, teasingly, "Three wickets for a duck!"

"We weren't out. They were all grounders!" came floating down the stairs from the bedroom.

Daddy went upstairs and peeped in where the three cricketers were lying.

"Next time," he said quietly, "why not take it in good part and say, 'Well bowled!' That would be ever so much more sportsmanlike."

"That's all right," said George, "but we weren't out."

"They were all grounders," shouted Tom.

"You bowled me too fast," cried Tim.

"Hopeless!" sighed Daddy, closing the door again. But as he reached the bottom of the stairs he couldn't resist one parting shot: "Three wickets for a duck!"

There was an answering growl from above and then silence.

But it never happened quite the same again.

Winter on the farm.

© Topical

In His Steps

THE Stanfords lived on a farm in the north of Scotland where, in winter, it becomes very cold and the snowfall is sometimes several feet in depth.

One morning as the family came downstairs they noticed that the kitchen was very dark. Someone pulled up the blind, but it made little difference.

"Why," said one of the boys, "the snow is actually above the window!"

And so it was. They all ran into the other rooms and found that the windows on one side of the house were quite blocked up, while even beneath the others there were several feet of snow.

Ned and Bessie, who were on a visit, were rather frightened.

"How shall we get to school this morning?" asked Ned.

"We shall never be able to walk through this."

"We shan't even be able to open the front door," said Bessie. But the others only smiled.

"Oh yes, we shall," said Mr. Stanford, "but we shall all have to work hard to clear a way out."

They all took spades or shovels and began to work their hardest, and it was not long before they had cut a path through the drift that covered the front garden. Now all around them was a sea of white, stretching as far as the eye could reach, broken only by occasional trees and buildings in the distance. The schoolhouse, about a mile away, was just in sight, covered, like everything else, with its thick mantle of snow.

"Well, I don't see how we are going to get there even now," said Ned. "The snow is too soft to walk on. We should sink up to our necks in it."

"Wait and see," said Mr. Stanford, "you will get there all right. This isn't the first time it has snowed here."

Schooltime came at last, a little earlier than usual, though, because of the snow.

"Follow me," said Mr. Stanford. "Put your feet exactly where I place mine and you will be quite all right. See?"

With that he started forward, his big boots sinking deep in the snow but making a hard patch on which the children could walk in safety.

Ned and Bess and the others followed. They put their little legs down into the deep holes made by Mr. Stanford's boots and trudged on towards the school. It was very slow work, because the holes were so deep that it was a job to get out of them again once you had got in, especially for short legs, too. But Mr. Stanford strode forward, and the children hopped along behind him, until at last the schoolhouse was reached.

"So you see we have got here all right," said Mr. Stanford, smiling, as the last of the children arrived.

"What a job!" sighed Bessie, panting, for she wasn't used to such a strenuous way of going to school.

"I kept thinking I was going to fall over and sink in the snow," said Ned.

"Now you see how important it is to follow exactly in Father's footsteps," laughed Mr. Stanford.

"Yes," said Ned and Bessie together.

"And that is just how we should follow the Lord Jesus," Mr. Stanford went on. "He has gone before all of us and marked out a way. As long as we follow Him carefully, putting our feet just where His feet trod, we shall be kept from all sin's pitfalls."

"That reminds me of the memory verse we had the other day," said Ned. "'Christ also suffered for us, leaving us an example, that ye should follow His steps.'" 1 Peter 2:21.

"Exactly, that's right," said Mr. Stanford. "And now I'm sure you will never forget it after this experience."

"I'm sure we never shall," replied the children, as the school door opened and teacher called them in.

Studying Hard.

The boy Samuel praying. © Braun et Cie.

How Bobby's Prayer was Answered

BOBBY was just old enough to have a Meccano set of his own. He had been given one for his birthday a few weeks ago and was now struggling to make up one of the patterns in the book. It was rather a difficult task for him, for his chubby fingers were so small they wouldn't pick up the screws easily; but he was carrying on with much patience and determination.

While Bobby and his Meccano set were sprawled out all over the dining-room table, Mamma was in the kitchen washing up the dishes after tea.

After a while she heard someone talking in the other room, and as she knew no one else was in the house except Bobby she stopped her work to listen.

"There's nuffin' in it, there's nuffin' in it," she heard a little voice say. "I knew there was nuffin' in it."

Mamma left the sink and peeped through the crack of the dining-room door. To her astonishment she saw Bobby just getting up off his knees, and heard him saying again to himself, "There's nuffin' in it."

Curiosity got the better of her and she went into the room.

"Nothing in what?" she asked.

"In prayer," said Bobby solemnly.

"Bobby dear!" exclaimed Mamma, "what do you mean?"

"I asked God to help me make this thing go right, and He hasn't done it," said Bobby.

Mamma would like to have smiled, but daren't. This was too serious a matter.

"Well, darling," she said, "sometimes God doesn't answer prayers immediately. Some people have to wait a long time for their prayers to be answered, but He always answers them sometime."

Bobby grunted as though he did not agree with this explanation of the ways of God.

"Perhaps, darling," said Mamma, "you have done enough for to-night. Why not leave it till the morning and go to bed? Maybe it will be easier then."

Bobby, who was really very tired, thought this was not such a bad idea after all, and putting all the pieces back into the box, he went upstairs to bed.

He said his prayers as usual, and although he had announced so definitely that there was "nuffin' in it" he asked God once more to help him fix his Meccano in the morning.

When he had gone to sleep, Mamma had a happy thought. She had never worked with a Meccano set in her life, but she got it out and started to carry on with the job Bobby had begun. Never had her fingers felt so clumsy as when she tried to get the little nuts to fit on the bolts, and more than once she hurt her fingers with the screw-driver. Slowly but surely, however, the pieces went together and Mamma began to get really interested and to wonder why she had not become an engineer instead of a mother.

At last the toy was finished, and with great care

Mamma carried it upstairs and placed it where Bobby could see it when he should wake in the morning.

Morning came, and Bobby, opening his eyes, shrieked with delight.

"Mamma, Mamma!" he called at the top of his voice. "Come quickly and see what's on my bed."

Mamma ran in, all smiles.

"Look, Mamma," he cried. "See, God did answer my prayer after all."

"Yes," said Mamma, "isn't that wonderful!"

Bobby looked thoughtful for a moment.

"I say, Mamma," he said, "did you put this together?"

"Why—er—yes," said Mamma hesitatingly. "I did it last night after you had gone to sleep."

"Then it wasn't God after all," said Bobby, with a trace of disappointment in his voice.

"Oh yes, it was," said Mamma, "because, you see, He made me think about doing it, and He helped me such a lot, too."

"Oh," grunted Bobby, not quite sure yet.

"Anyway," said Mamma, "that's why God gives little boys mammas—just to help Him answer their prayers."

© Franz Hanfstaengl

"He calleth His own sheep by name."

The Wrong Baby

BABY JEAN had been away in hospital for several weeks and her home had been very lonely without her. Every evening when Daddy came back from work his first question would be, "Any news about Jean?" and Mother would go down to the hospital at least once a day to ask how she was getting on.

Imagine their joy when one morning a letter arrived from the Matron to say that Jean was now well enough to leave the hospital and the ambulance would bring her home the next day.

At last the great moment came. The ambulance drew up at the door and Mother rushed out, her face radiant with smiles, to welcome her darling Jean.

"Here she is, back again at last," said the nurse kindly, gently lifting the little child and placing her in Mother's arms.

"Isn't it just lovely to have her home again?" said Mother, hugging the child closer still, and running indoors.

When evening came, Daddy was just as happy. He picked her up and nursed her on his lap all the time he was eating his supper.

Yet there was something not quite right. Mother had noticed it first, but Daddy soon saw it, too.

"Jean seems to have changed a little since she has been away," he said, as the two sat by the fire after the child had been put to bed.

"I thought so, too," said Mother. "She is so re-
served, I simply can't get any love out of her at all,
and she cries such a lot."

"That's what I noticed," said Daddy, "she just
sits still and looks at me in a surprised, frightened
sort of way. But I suppose she will get over it soon.
Probably it's because she has been away so long."

"Perhaps so," said Mother, rather uncertainly.

There was a pause for a few minutes.

"I suppose," said Mother presently, "you are sure
it is Jean?"

"Why, bless me, I suppose so!" exclaimed Daddy.
"Why, do you think there has been a mistake?"

The two walked upstairs and looked at the sleeping child. The features were Jean's exactly, the nose
just as stubby, the hair just as fair and curly, and the
ears stood out in just the same way. Of course, it
must be Jean. But Mother wasn't quite sure yet.

They waited another day. Mother did all she could
to show the child how much she loved her, but nothing
she did seemed to break the barrier of shyness. The
little one cried almost without cessation. By the time
Daddy came home the next afternoon she was beginning to get desperate.

"I'm more sure than ever there has been a mistake," she said. "I'm going down to the hospital right
away."

"Well—er—" began Daddy, but Mother was
gone.

Arriving at the hospital, she asked to see the
Matron and told of her suspicions.

"Impossible! Quite impossible!" affirmed the
Matron. "It could never happen."

But Mother was insistent and demanded to be allowed to go to the children's ward, and at last the Matron consented.

There seemed to be scores of babies there of all sorts and descriptions, some of them lying in their little cots, others sitting up, and some toddling about. Mother walked among them from one end of the ward to the other, calling out, "Jean, Jean!" Most of them took no notice of her at all, while some peeped shyly at the Matron. A few gave little smiles of welcome. But there was no Jean.

They had almost reached the end of the ward, and Mother was just telling herself that she had been very foolish, when a voice was heard from one of the last cots, "Mamma! Mamma!" It was Jean.

There could be no mistake about this. The little child stretched up her baby arms and Mother sprang towards her with tears of joy running down her cheeks.

What a dreadful mistake had nearly happened! And what rejoicing there was at home when it was all put right again.

And by a strange coincidence, as Daddy was reading to Mother that night from the good old Book, he happened on these words: "And the sheep hear His voice: and He calleth His own sheep by name, and leadeth them out. . . . For they know His voice. And a stranger will they not follow, but will flee from him: for they know not the voice of strangers." John 10: 3-5.

"Do you know," he said, "I don't think I ever saw quite so much in those words before."

"No," said Mother, "and I never did, too."

Saved by His Dog

JOE was down at the lakeside with his sisters and their little friends having a very jolly time. Most of them were paddling and some were fishing.

Joe, although only four years old, was a very brave boy and he was wading out with the others just as far as his baby legs would take him—or rather just as far as his breeches would let him, for he had been told not to get them wet.

Romping about with all the children was Rover, Joe's pet dog. A fine collie he was, full of fun, and as fond of Joe as Joe was of him.

All of a sudden Joe, wading out in a new direction, stepped into a deep hole and disappeared beneath the water. One of the girls saw him go under and immediately raised a scream which was soon taken up by all the rest.

No one knew what to do next and two or three rushed away across the fields to find Joe's father and mother. The rest stood on the bank, alternately crying and screaming.

The only one that kept his head was Rover. He took in the situation at a glance and with a mighty plunge dashed to the rescue of his little chum. With swift strokes of his big paws he swam towards the spot where Joe had gone down and as the poor little chap rose to the surface again Rover seized him in his powerful jaws and began swimming towards the bank.

As he reached it and clambered out, some of the children ran forward to take Joe from him, but Rover, perhaps realizing their helplessness, pushed them away and marched on, with Joe in his jaws, towards the boy's home. He had actually carried him across two fields before he met Joe's parents running towards the lake. They were both panting and very frightened, feeling sure that their precious Joe must have been drowned. Their surprise at seeing the curious bundle in Rover's mouth can be imagined.

As for Rover, he dropped his burden gently in front of the parents and then stood by whimpering, as though not sure whether he had rescued the boy in time or not.

The distracted parents dropped by the boy's side and tried to restore him to consciousness. The task took them some time, but their efforts were rewarded. At last Joe opened his eyes and they knew all was well.

How happy everybody was then, but none so much as Rover. You should have just seen his tail wagging as he led the triumphal procession back to the house —and his kennel. He had done his duty and was justly proud. And the supper he had that night exceeded any that he had ever imagined in his wildest doggie dreams.

Pussy finds a friend.

© Fox Photos

The Boy Who Said, "Garn!"

HAVING told you about the boy who was saved by his dog, I must tell you another story of the cat who was saved by a boy—and both these incidents happened since the last series of BEDTIME STORIES was written!

Well, this poor cat had got lost in London. Perhaps it was the noise, or the crowds of people, or the dozens and dozens of streets, leading seemingly in all directions, that had bewildered her. Anyway, she was lost.

Thinking that perhaps if she were to cross the road she might find her way back home, she made a dive into the traffic, dodging here and there and doing her very best to get to the other side. But it was all too much for her. She felt as though she had become a mouse and all these huge machines were chasing her, determined to kill her if possible.

Oh dear! What a near thing that was! The wheel of a bus almost grazed her nose.

Phew! A taxicab dashed past, nearly shaving off her whiskers. Would she never get across? Death seemed very near, and nobody seemed to care. She looked this way and that, not knowing whether to go forward or backward, and meanwhile she was sure another bus was coming straight towards her. Someone was shouting, "Get out of the way!" and some-one else, "Mind that cat!"

Then suddenly, when almost under the very bon-net of the bus, a little ragged figure jumped towards her, picked her up in his strong arms, and leaped back in a flash on to the pavement.

It was only a poor newspaper boy, but she felt she loved him very much for his great kindness. No one else had thought of helping her in her desperate need. He placed her gently on the pavement and she meowed contentedly at his feet.

Just then a big gentleman came up to the boy. He looked as though he must be a lord, or at least a mem-ber of Parliament.

"That was a very brave deed, my boy," said he. "I would like you to give me your name and address, for you deserve a medal for this."

"Garn!" said the boy.

"I really mean it," said the big gentleman. "Wouldn't you like a medal?"

"Garn!" repeated the lad. "Mother told us we had to be kind to animals and not to expect any re-ward."

And with that the boy turned and bolted, leaving the big gentleman and the poor little pussy to stare at each other in surprise!

The Bird With the Kindly Heart

HERE is the prettiest bird story I think I have ever heard. It's about a little chaffinch that lived—and may still live, for aught I know—at Saundersfoot in Pembrokeshire.

Saundersfoot, by the way, is a dear little seaside village, with just a few old-fashioned houses and a delightful stretch of sandy beach. A long lane, running between flower-decked hedgerows, separates it from the nearest railway station. I know, because I went there once in search of a friend—and found he had left two hours before I got there! I also missed the chaffinch, and of that I am more sorry still.

One stormy day not very long ago this little bird, wearied perhaps by the wind, flew through an open window into one of the houses in the village.

Now it so happened that in the room was a little invalid girl, Kathleen by name, who was delighted to see her little visitor. She gave it some food and cared for it tenderly all the night till the storm was over. Then in the morning the chaffinch flew away.

But the next day, to Kathleen's surprise and delight, it returned, took some food, and flew away again! The next day it did the same, and for quite a time there was not a morning passed but the chaffinch turned up for its breakfast.

© Topical

A chaffinch.

Then one day the visits ceased, and poor Kathleen thought the bird must surely have been killed. She waited and waited, keeping some food close to the window, but in vain.

A week later, however, the chaffinch turned up again, but with a wound in its little breast. Kathleen was very sorry for it and nursed it till it was well again, watching it eat from a tiny tray on her bed. They became fast friends.

Then an extraordinary thing happened. One day Kathleen's aunt came into the room while the little girl was asleep and saw a strange piece of ribbon lying on her hair. She wondered how ever it could have come there, and Kathleen, when she woke up, said she knew nothing about it.

But the next day the aunt found a piece of pink gauze lying against the child's cheek. They were now thoroughly puzzled, but as they were talking about it, in through the open window flew the chaffinch with another little gift—this time a piece of blue ribbon, in its beak. It dropped the ribbon on the pillow and flew away.

After that this dear little bird with the kindly heart brought, among other gifts, some lace, a snail's shell, some thistledown, a tiny piece of bracken, some coloured wool, and a small curtain ring.

What a lesson in gratitude! Evidently the chaffinch was trying in its feeble way to say, "Thank you," for all the sick girl's kindness. And as I heard the story I thought of the Master's words, "She hath done what she could!"

A Brave Little Girl

TALKING about birds reminds me of another true bird story with a really thrilling adventure.

Dick, a very pretty canary, belonged to a little girl called Minnie, who lived in the country with her father and mother.

Dick had been a birthday present to Minnie and she loved him very much indeed. Although she had a beautiful golden cage for him, yet Dick was often allowed out and would perch on Minnie's shoulder, or on the side of her plate at mealtimes. Minnie had only to whistle quietly to start Dick off in a riot of glorious song that filled the whole house with music.

Then one day Dick disappeared. His cage door was open, and no Dick was to be seen. Minnie searched the house from top to bottom, but all in vain. Then she went out into the garden and peered into all the bushes, listening for any little "Cheep, cheep!" that might reveal the presence of her precious birdie. But still no Dick was to be found.

Minnie talked very seriously to the dog and the cat. Indeed she had grave suspicions about them, especially pussy, but both professed absolute innocence.

Three days passed, and still no Dick appeared. Poor little Minnie was heart-broken, for she felt that never again would she be able to get a bird so tame and loving as her dear little Dick.

84

Then one morning a neighbour called. "I think I know where your canary is," she said.

"Do you really?" cried Minnie. "Where, where?"

"Come with me and I will show you," said the neighbour. "I think I heard him calling."

"Let's go at once," said Minnie, dashing out of the house and dragging the neighbour with her.

"This way," said the lady, walking in the direction of the well. They reached the edge and looked over, Minnie holding tightly to the neighbour's hand. "Listen!"

They both listened. Then from far down in the darkness they heard a faint "Cheep! cheep!"

"It's Dick, it's Dick!" cried Minnie. "My poor little Dick! However shall we get him out?"

"Let's go and tell Father," said the neighbour. "Perhaps he will think of a way."

They both ran back to the house.

"We've found him!" cried Minnie. "He is down at the bottom of the well. How shall we get him out?"

"I'm afraid it's impossible," said Father. "It's very deep, and I haven't a ladder nearly long enough to reach to the bottom."

"But we can't leave Dick there," cried Minnie. "Let me go down and fetch him."

"You go down the well!" cried Father.

"Yes, I'll go. You let me down in the bucket, then I'll pick him up and you can pull me to the top again."

"We couldn't do that," said Father.

"But we must," said Minnie. "It will be quite all right. Do, Daddy, come on! Let's go now before Dick dies."

Minnie was so in earnest that Father relented and

the three walked over to the well together. Again they looked down the deep, dark hole.

"Are you sure you want to go down there?" said Father.

"Yes, yes, of course," said brave little Minnie. "Can't you hear Dick calling me?"

Then without another word she stepped into the bucket. Father tied the rope very tightly around her, so that there was no possibility of her slipping out. Then, very, very carefully, he lowered her over the edge.

Down, down, down, went Minnie. Oh, how dark it was! But as she descended so Dick's little "Cheep! cheep!" became louder and louder. It seemed as though he guessed Minnie was coming to his rescue. And Minnie didn't mind the dark a bit for she was so anxious to save her little friend.

Splash! At last the bucket touched the water and Father stopped paying out the rope.

"Dick! Dick!" cried Minnie, peering through the darkness. Yes, there was the poor, frightened little bird, perched on a little ledge on the side of the well. She reached out her hands with joy and picked him up, signalling to her father to pull them both to the top again.

Up, up, up, they went together, and at last they were out in the sunshine once again and Father was clasping his brave little girl in his arms.

"But weren't you afraid?" he said to her.

"Of course I wasn't!" she replied. "I knew you were holding the rope."

"Well," said Father, as he was telling the story at home that evening, "I hope we shall always trust our heavenly Father as Minnie trusted me."

A Story That Isn't True

I DON'T mean that my story isn't true. On the con-
trary it is very true indeed. You see, I know the boy
concerned very well, and he wouldn't tell a fib to save
his life. I'm going to call him Donald just so you won't
know who he is.

Donald brought the story in question home from
school one day and told his Daddy what he had heard.

It was like this:

In the history class the teacher wanted to begin
right at the beginning of things and so he told this
curious tale. He said that life began on this world as
a tiny speck of some sort of slimy stuff in the sea. This
tiny speck gradually grew and grew and then broke
up, part of it deciding to become a fish, part of it becoming a plant, and part of it crawling up on the land
and turning into a worm.

From this first fish, this first plant, and this first
little worm, all the fishes and all the plants and all the
animals have come. At least, so the teacher said. Then
he went on to try to trace the history of the worm
until at last, after billions and billions of years, it became a more important animal.

This worm, he said, as it began to crawl on its
tummy, developed a wart, and this wart became a leg.
Some worms got four warts and so they grew four
legs. Others got lots of warts and so they turned into
centipedes.

© Topical

Some monkeys may be very clever but they never turn into men.

Animals got eyes, he said, because as the light of the sun played upon them, a freckle came out which after a while turned into an eye.

Then as millions of years passed some of the worms that had developed legs from their warts became dogs, some of them became cats, some of them leopards, and some lions, tigers, giraffes, and so on.

One set of worms worked along, so the teacher stated, until it had grown arms as well as legs, and became monkeys.

The more advanced monkeys were playing about with some sticks one day when they accidentally rubbed them together and made the first spark of fire. So after that they were able to light fires when they wanted to, and gradually, because of the extra warmth, their hair fell off and they turned into men!

Well, that was briefly the story the teacher told Donald in school, and a grammar school at that. It is a story that is being told to children all over the country to-day, indeed in all the world. But it is not a true story. In fact I feel like calling it a wicked lie.

It is not true, because God has told us in the Bible that He created all things. They did not "evolve" through millions and billions of years from a speck of slime in the sea. He made them all Himself by His own wisdom and might. As we read in the Psalms: "By the Word of the Lord were the heavens made; and all the host of them by the breath of His mouth. . . . For He spake, and it was done; He commanded, and it stood fast." Psa. 33:6, 9.

As for man himself, we are told: "So God created man in His own image, in the image of God created

He him; male and female created He them." Gen.
1:27.

And, after all, how very silly is this untrue story
that is being told to so many boys and girls to-day!
If you stop to think about it for but a few minutes you
just have to laugh.

Take that first speck of slime in the sea. Who put
it there? Who made the sea for it to grow in? Who
made the land on to which that first worm crawled
when it got tired of being in the sea?

Then think of those poor little worms with the
warts on their tummies. Why did they get the warts
in the right places so that the legs came where they
would be useful? And why didn't they get still more
warts on their legs as well—and so have them stick-
ing out in all directions?

It's all too silly for words, isn't it? But think about
those eyes. Oh dear! The sun kept playing on a freckle
until an eye came out, they say. But why did it choose
a freckle beside the animal's nose? And then choose
another freckle on the other side of its nose? Why
didn't it choose a freckle on the back of its head, or
on its legs, or possibly on its tail? Indeed, why didn't
eyes start bobbing out all over its body?

And then, if it really was the rays of the sun that
caused the freckles to turn into eyes, why didn't they
make them strong enough to bear the light? Why,
after making eyes, did they form eyelids to keep the
light out?

And now we come to those poor monkeys who are
supposed to have turned into men. They lost their
hair because they discovered fire and so didn't need
it any more! Did they indeed! Why, then, didn't they

lose it off their heads at the same time? And why don't cats lose their hair nowadays when they sleep by the fire? And why do monkeys that live in hot countries still have their hair to-day?

No, children, this story that is going around is neither true nor sensible. It has been made up by people who do not love the Bible and are trying to find some other explanation of how things came on this earth. And if you ask me, I think that it is a thousand times more difficult to believe than the simple Bible story of creation. Donald thinks so, too.

God's Champions

HAVE you ever had someone take your part when you were "up against it" in an argument or a "scrap"? Wasn't it encouraging to find someone willing to stand by you and maintain your cause?

Perhaps some boys were trying to tease you. Maybe they were knocking your cap off and throwing stones at you and calling you names and then, just as you were beginning to get really scared, another boy suddenly appeared and said, "Stop it now! Leave him alone or I'll go for you!" What a thrill! And didn't you feel grateful to your friend?

Or perhaps you are a little girl and some of the others in your class were sneering at you because you would not get up to some mischief they were planning. Perhaps they were calling you a "Mother's darling" and all that sort of thing, when another girl came on the scene and said, "She's right, girls, I'm not going to do it either. If she's a 'Mother's darling,' so am I." And then you felt all stirred up inside, didn't you, and you wanted to throw your arms around the girl who had so bravely stood by your side.

We all love the boys and girls who champion the cause of the weak and helpless, and stand up against all odds for the right. They grow up to be fine men and women of whom the world is justly proud.

Looking back over history, who were some of the greatest men who ever lived? Some would mention

Napoleon or Wellington and other men who led the armies of the nations to battle. But were not men like Wilberforce and Livingstone greater far than they?

You have heard, of course, of Wilberforce. He it was who championed the cause of the slaves. He said that it was a disgrace to the British Empire that any one of the king's subjects should be held in slavery, and both in and out of Parliament he laboured to arouse the conscience of the people to stop this terrible evil. And he succeeded, too, for all the slaves were freed at last.

Livingstone, also, was a champion of the weak. He came back from Africa with his heart on fire because of the wicked things he had seen being done to the poor natives of that country, and largely because of his self-sacrificing, pioneer work a new day dawned for them.

Then there was Florence Nightingale. She heard of the sufferings of the poor soldiers in the Crimean war and went out bravely to nurse them. They called her "the lady of the lamp" because she carried a little lamp with her as she went round visiting the sick and wounded. Largely because of what she did we have the splendid hospitals of to-day with their staffs of well-trained nurses.

Maybe you have heard of Elizabeth Fry. In days when prisons were much worse places than they are now, she championed the cause of the suffering prisoners, and as a result of her work great reforms were introduced.

Old General Booth was another such champion. His heart was touched by all the hardship and distress of the poor and he started his Salvation Army

chiefly to help them. How great a boon this has been
to the poor in all the world everybody knows now.

Then there was Dr. Barnado, who conceived the
idea of taking care of poor orphan children. He
adopted as the motto for his home, "No destitute
child ever refused admission." Tens of thousands of
children have since had cause to thank him for the
largeness of his loving heart.

Such as these were the world's greatest men and
women. When the names of kings and generals have
been forgotten, theirs will shine on with radiance
through eternal years.

For all who champion the cause of the poor and
needy are indeed the champions of God. He identifies
Himself with them. Although He Himself possesses
all the treasures of heaven, He says that those who
show kindness to the hungry, the thirsty, the sick, and
the prisoners are really helping Him.

When Jesus comes back again He will say to all
His champions: "Come, ye blessed of My Father, in-
herit the kingdom prepared for you from the foundation of the world: for I was an hungred, and ye gave
Me meat: I was thirsty, and ye gave Me drink: I was
a stranger, and ye took Me in: naked, and ye clothed
Me: I was sick, and ye visited Me: I was in prison,
and ye came unto Me."

Then shall His champions say to Him: "Lord,
when saw we Thee an hungred, and fed Thee? or
thirsty, and gave Thee drink? When saw we Thee a
stranger, and took thee in? or naked, and clothed
Thee? Or when saw we Thee sick, or in prison, and
came unto Thee?

"And the King shall answer and say unto them,

Verily I say unto you, Inasmuch as ye have done it unto one of the least of these My brethren, ye have done it unto Me." Matt. 25:34-40.

One may be God's champion, too, not only by helping the weak and helpless, but by standing for the right. To refuse to tell a lie, to speak up boldly for the Bible when someone is sneering at it, to refuse to disobey one of God's commandments, is to be one of His noble champions.

Daniel was such an one. After the king's decree that any who should be found at prayer should be cast into the den of lions, it took a brave man to continue. But Daniel, we are told, "his windows being open in his chamber towards Jerusalem, he kneeled upon his knees three times a day, and prayed, and gave thanks before his God, as he did aforetime." Dan. 6:10. The thought of the den of lions made no difference to him. As God's chosen champion he knew there was nothing else for him to do at that time than to go on praying.

I think Paul was one of God's champions, too. He tells us that he received one hundred and ninety-five lashes, was three times beaten with rods, was once stoned and three times shipwrecked, yet he never ceased his witness for his Master. With wonderful courage he said: "We are troubled on every side, yet not distressed; we are perplexed, but not in despair; persecuted, but not forsaken; cast down, but not destroyed." 2 Cor. 4:8, 9. There was a hero, if you like! And he suffered all that he might champion the cause of God. I am sure God will have some special reward for him in His kingdom.

And God is looking for champions to-day. The

eyes of the Lord that "run to and fro through the whole earth" are seeking for boys and girls who will give their hearts to Him and stand firmly for righteousness and truth amid all the evil of these modern times. He wants them to keep His commandments and to witness boldly for Jesus. He wants them to do right when alone, at school, at play, not only because it is right, but because they belong to Him.

Have you heard His call? To every boy and girl He says to-day, "Give Me thine heart." He wants to make us all strong and wise and good. He wants to fill us with His Holy Spirit and make us His own chosen champions. Shall we let Him? And shall we do it now?

NOTE.—There are now nine series of BEDTIME STORIES. The companion volumes may be obtained at 1/- each, or any five numbers for 4/- from the printers and publishers:

The Stanborough Press Ltd., Watford, Herts.

10M/54/233